The Rise of Adolf Hitler

The Rise of
Adolf Hitler

Other books in the At Issue in History series:

The Rise of
Adolf Hitler

Annette Dufner, *Book Editor*

Daniel Leone, *President*
Bonnie Szumski, *Publisher*
Scott Barbour, *Managing Editor*

 AT ISSUE IN HISTORY

GREENHAVEN
PRESS ®

San Diego • Detroit • New York • San Francisco • Cleveland
New Haven, Conn. • Waterville, Maine • London • Munich

© 2003 by Greenhaven Press. Greenhaven Press is an imprint of The Gale Group, Inc., a division of Thomson Learning, Inc.

Greenhaven® and Thomson Learning™ are trademarks used herein under license.

For more information, contact
Greenhaven Press
27500 Drake Rd.
Farmington Hills, MI 48331-3535
Or you can visit our Internet site at http://www.gale.com

LIBRARY OF CONGRESS CATALOGING-IN-PUBLICATION DATA
The rise of Adolf Hitler / Annette Dufner, book editor.
p. cm. — (At issue in history)
Includes bibliographical references and index.
ISBN 0-7377-1518-9 (lib. : alk. paper) — ISBN 0-7377-1519-7 (pbk. : alk. paper)
1. Hitler, Adolf, 1889–1945. 2. Heads of state—Germany—Biography.
3. Germany—Politics and government—1933–1945. 4. National socialism.
I. Dufner, Annette. II. Series.
DD247.H5 R57 2003
943.086'092—dc21   2002190704

Printed in the United States of America

Contents

Chapter 1: Political and Social Conditions That Contributed to Hitler's Rise

gave more and more power to the police and
finally infringed on citizens' rights to protection
under the law.

Chapter 3: The World Responds

Foreword

Historian Robert Weiss defines history simply as "a record and interpretation of past events." Both elements—record and interpretation—are necessary, Weiss argues.

> Names, dates, places, and events are the essence of history. But historical writing is not a compendium of facts. It consists of facts placed in a sequence to tell a connected story. A work of history is not merely a story, however. It also must analyze what happened and *why*—that is, it must interpret the past for the reader.

For example, the events of December 7, 1941, that led President Franklin D. Roosevelt to call it "a date which will live in infamy" are fairly well known and straightforward. A force of Japanese planes and submarines launched a torpedo and bombing attack on American military targets in Pearl Harbor, Hawaii. The surprise assault sank five battleships, disabled or sank fourteen additional ships, and left almost twenty-four hundred American soldiers and sailors dead. On the following day, the United States formally entered World War II when Congress declared war on Japan.

These facts and consequences were almost immediately communicated to the American people who heard reports about Pearl Harbor and President Roosevelt's response on the radio. All realized that this was an important and pivotal event in American and world history. Yet the news from Pearl Harbor raised many unanswered questions. Why did Japan decide to launch such an offensive? Why were the attackers so successful in catching America by surprise? What did the attack reveal about the two nations, their people, and their leadership? What were its causes, and what were its effects? Political leaders, academic historians, and students look to learn the basic facts of historical events and to read the intepretations of these events by many different sources, both primary and secondary, in order to develop a more complete picture of the event in a historical context.

In the case of Pearl Harbor, several important questions surrounding the event remain in dispute, most notably the role of President Roosevelt. Some historians have blamed his policies for deliberately provoking Japan to attack in order to propel America into World War II; a few have gone so far as to accuse him of knowing of the impending attack but not informing others. Other historians, examining the same event, have exonerated the president of such charges, arguing that the historical evidence does not support such a theory.

The Greenhaven At Issue in History series recognizes that many important historical events have been interpreted differently and in some cases remain shrouded in controversy. Each volume features a collection of articles that focus on a topic that has sparked controversy among eyewitnesses, contemporary observers, and historians. An introductory essay sets the stage for each topic by presenting background and context. Several chapters then examine different facets of the subject at hand with readings chosen for their diversity of opinion. Each selection is preceded by a summary of the author's main points and conclusions. A bibliography is included for those students interested in pursuing further research. An annotated table of contents and thorough index help readers to quickly locate material of interest. Taken together, the contents of each of the volumes in the Greenhaven At Issue in History series will help students become more discriminating and thoughtful readers of history.

Introduction

How Adolf Hitler could have gained the portentous power he did remains one of the most puzzling questions in the history of the twentieth century. Historians, political scientists, and others have expended tremendous effort in their attempts to understand the rise of Hitler and the Nazis, but it remains disturbing that an individual man could gain enough support among the German population to darken the world with a war that left tens of millions of soldiers and civilians dead. Furthermore, the Nazi regime encumbered history with the brutal industrialized extinction of millions for their political convictions, for their disabilities, for their sexual orientation and—in particular—for their ethnicity and religion. It is not clear whether this is what the Germans wanted, or whether they were tricked into cooperation by a devious illusionist. Most historians agree, however, that Hitler's rise to power was enabled by the terrible meeting of a desperate, vulnerable population and a driven ideologue bent on achieving power and implementing his radical agenda.

In a span of fewer than ten years, Hitler went from being a troublesome but largely powerless distraction to the German government to being, for all intents and purposes, *the* German government. Along the way the Weimar Republic, the first democracy in German history, was replaced with an absolute dictatorship in which Hitler's word alone was law. Hitler's rise, however, was not a coup d'état, in which an individual or group seizes power in one swift moment. Instead, Hitler assumed absolute control over Germany through a series of small but significant steps.

The Problems of the Weimar Democracy

Hitler's rise was abetted by various problems that plagued the Weimar government established following Germany's defeat in World War I. One of those problems was a lack of popular support for the government itself. At the time of their country's surrender, many Germans thought they were actually winning the war, as their troops were still far beyond the previous German borders. The citizens of Germany saw little sign of impending defeat until they were suddenly struck with the news that a peace treaty had been signed at Versailles announcing that Germany had lost and that it alone bore responsibility for the outbreak of the war. Although it seems clear now that there was no way Germany could have won the war, at the time, the so-called stab-in-the-back myth swept the country. According to this theory, the politicians in the homeland had betrayed their own soldiers who were still bravely fighting at the front. The founders and early supporters of the Weimar democracy were called "the November criminals" because of the armistice that had been signed in November 1918. This inflammatory term was used by all sorts of political groups, including the Nazis. The perceived injustice of national humiliation was deepened by reparation demands upon Germany to pay large sums in currency and goods to the Allies.

Even before ordinary Germans could recover from the shock of sudden defeat, leftist uprisings rattled the country. On the very day that the Weimar democracy was founded, Socialists and Communists, led by the leftist revolutionary Karl Liebknecht, proclaimed a counter-regime. Street battles ensued between the troops of the republic and Liebknecht's followers. Eventually, the government fled from the volatile capital of Berlin to settle in nearby Weimar. But the revolts continued throughout the country. Because the Weimar government was the first democracy in Germany's history, people lacked understanding of the processes by which democratic decisions are made. The various parties within the parliament often acted more like lobby groups and demonstrated a lack of ability to channel public debate in such a manner as to achieve consensus. Even Germany's intellectuals showed little hope and less enthusiasm for the new form of government, and the Weimar chancellors soon turned to using emergency decrees to bypass their estranged, deadlocked coalition governments.

The political problems that plagued Germany were no match, however, for economic crises that choked the nation through much of the 1920s. Although there was little prosperity after the close of World War I, the situation became more grave in January 1923, when French and Belgian troops marched into the Ruhr, one of Germany's most important industrial areas, ostensibly because the struggling country was behind in its reparations payments. Bloody fighting broke out between the German workers and the occupying soldiers; workers who went on strike and wanted to prevent the French and Belgians from taking their paychecks were executed. There was outrage throughout Germany, and the government told the workers in the Ruhr region to go on general strike.

This led to a hyperdeflation of the German currency that deprived many Germans of their life savings. By September 5, 1923, for example, one could buy 16 million marks with 1 dollar. The very next day, the dollar was already worth 33,333,333 marks, and the price of a loaf of bread in Berlin rose to 1 million marks. People soon went grocery shopping with wheelbarrows full of paper money that they picked up from their spouses at the factory doors during lunch hour. Time was literally money: In the evenings the money was already worth so much less that some used it to fire their stoves. Private banks produced more and more paper money; often new numbers were simply printed onto the old bills. Finally, in November, the currency was replaced by the preliminary Rentenmark.

This new currency, as well as the decision to end the passive resistance in the Ruhr, led to a period of relative stability. But just six years later, in 1929, the Great Depression struck. Germany's welfare system was soon faced with unemployment rates of up to 30 percent. Desperate job seekers wandered the streets wearing signs saying: "I will take any kind of work." For the second time in only a few years Germans had to watch their country's economy crash and the fruits of their personal labor go to waste. Often, because of the disparity in wages due to gender, lesser-paid women were employed while their husbands were not, and the reversal of traditional roles added private tensions.

The economic despair of the Great Depression, just a few years after the record hyperdeflation of the German currency, spread poverty and mass unemployment throughout the country. In the face of such despair, few Germans were able to retain strong faith in the struggling democratic government that had been introduced by Germany's former enemies after World War I. To many who were hoping for a strong hand to bring the country back to order, Hitler's determined appearance and the hardheaded resolutions he put forth must have seemed like a worthwhile agenda geared to benefit the German people.

Hitler's Agenda

Oddly, the determination and leadership style Hitler projected were in stark contrast to those he had presented as he was coming of age. Before the war, the young Austrian had spent a few aimless years in Vienna and Munich, where he had lived the life of an unwashed, jobless tramp, living partly in shelters for homeless men after having been rejected by art academies in both cities. He volunteered for the German army in World War I, and he earned an Iron Cross and a promotion. However, he never became more than the equivalent of a private first class. After a mustard gas attack toward the end of the war, Hitler went temporarily blind. It was supposedly then that he finally received—or rather hallucinated—his "calling." He was to liberate Germany and make it free from the "Versailles dictate," from the "November state," and from what he saw as the ever-present source of decay within German racial purity: the Jew.

Back in Munich after the end of the war, Hitler held a job in the army that required him to watch small extremist parties. One of them was the German Workers' Party (DAP), which then had only seven members. Hitler liked their undeveloped rightist agenda and he joined the group. Soon the other party members realized the potential Hitler held for their party: His rally speeches began to attract thousands of listeners, and people seemed to be fascinated by his pathos. The party grew dramatically. Shortly after his talent was discovered, Hitler was made the leader of the party and granted almost dictatorial privileges. He merged the party with other right-wing groups, and the National Socialist Workers' Party (NSDAP), also called the Nazi Party, emerged. Then, in 1923, the anti-Semite made his first go for big politics. Together with some friends, he initiated and executed the so-called Beer Hall Putsch, a semi-improvised coup that started in a Munich bar in an attempt to overthrow the republic and set up a new regime. The fanatical and badly organized attempt failed miserably, however, and Hitler was arrested and thrown into prison. There he had time to write his notorious book *Mein Kampf (My Struggle)*, which outlines the core of his radical agenda.

Few guessed at the time that Hitler was anything more than a small-time political aspirant. Indeed, when Hitler was released from prison after just half a year, the American public could read the following reassuring lines about him in a small article buried deep inside the *New York Times:*

> He looked a much sadder and wiser man today than last Spring when he, with Ludendorff and other radical extremists, appeared before a Munich court charged with conspiracy to overthrow the Government. His behavior during imprisonment convinced the authorities that [he and] his political organization . . . was no longer to be feared. It is believed he will retire to private life and return to Austria, the country of his birth.

The true wisdom that Hitler had gained in prison, however, was that if his radical agenda was to succeed he needed the support of the masses. The next time, therefore, he would try to come to power using ostensibly legal and democratic means rather than violent rebellion. And he had the details of his program ready: His intention was war and the extinction of "European Jewry." The purified, strong, and fertile Aryan race would need more living space, he was convinced. The plan to annex and occupy Germany's eastern neighbors had already taken firm shape in his mind.

As Germany's economic situation continued to worsen during those postwar years, the message in Hitler's oratory came to represent the people's hope. And with his leadership of the Nazi Party undisputed, it would take less than a decade for him to be in a position to implement his agenda.

The Chain of Events

On July 31, 1932, Hitler could be confident his plan was working. On that day, he and his Nazi Party gained 37.4 percent of the vote in a federal election. This result meant that in less than two years the Nazis had managed to nearly double the number of seats they held in the German parliament. Hitler and the Nazis suffered a setback in the November 1932 election, though when they gained just 33.1 percent of the vote. In fact, they never won more than 43.9 percent of the vote. However, this inability to achieve an absolute majority in parliament did not keep them from taking complete control of the country. Historians sometimes discuss the election results in an attempt to figure out just how committed the German population was to the Nazi program and Hitler's blatant anti-Semitism. Their studies are hindered, however, by the fact that after 1933 democratic elections ceased.

In January of that year, Hitler became chancellor of Germany, an event celebrated by Nazis as "the seizure of power." Despite the grand term, it is more accurate to say that Hitler was handed power than that he seized it, for it was the aging president Paul von Hindenburg who appointed Hitler chancellor. Why did the president choose the anti-Semite instead of someone else? Many believe it was because Hindenburg, a former aristocratic military general raised in the Prussian tradition, appreciated Hitler's authoritative bent. As well, Hindenburg had seen several chancellors fail because they were unable to command a majority in their coalition governments. If Hindenburg had any reservations, he started to run out of options when even Hitler's competitor, the conservative Franz von Papen, pressured the president to choose Hitler.

Although Chancellor Hitler controlled less than one-half of the Parliament, an ominous terrorist attack—the exact circumstances of which remain opaque—soon allowed him to ask President Hindenburg for the right to rule by emergency decree. The basis of this practice, which had been adopted by several of Hitler's predecessors, was Article 48 of the Weimar Constitution, which let civil rights be suspended in times of national emergency. This article is often referred to as the dictatorship article and pointed to as one of the structural weaknesses of the Weimar democracy. On February 27, 1933, the parliament building was set on fire and burned down. Historians generally agree that the Dutchman Marinus van der Lubbe, who was arrested for setting the fire, may actually have been involved. However, the possibility continues to exist that it was the Nazis themselves who set the fire as an act of political intimidation. Conclusive evidence either way is lacking. Whatever the truth may be, Hitler and his party functionaries led the public to believe that the Communist Party was responsible for the fire, and the Nazis used the opportunity to pass the Reichstag Fire Decree and start eliminating the Bolsheviks, whom they hated, and, ultimately, the other Weimar parties. Within days, important Communist leaders were arrested or assassinated, and many others fled. Van der Lubbe, who was mentally challenged, was executed without a proper trial, and no investigation was pursued.

Soon after the fire in Parliament, Hitler landed the final blow in his fight for absolute control. By playing on fears of rebellion, he managed to push the so-called Enabling Act through Parliament. This law declared that henceforth Hitler was able to rule without parliamentary approval. It made him the only one in charge and brought a formal end to the democracy. For the most part, the elected representatives themselves ended the democracy, and it is indeed often claimed that the Weimar democracy committed suicide. Others say, however, that this last vote was not actually democratic because terror and coercion were already pervasive. By the end of 1933, the Weimar Republic, the first democracy in German history, had been replaced by the Third Reich, Germany's most ominous and deadly empire.

The Consequences

The end of parliamentary democracy was not enough for Hitler. He disempowered influential German organizations and replaced them with Nazi networks that were under his personal control. He was adamant there was to be no breeding ground for opposition. The Nazi Party remained the only legal party, and the independent labor unions were dissolved and replaced by a Nazi union that bribed workers with cheap vacations. A Nazi committee decided whether pieces of art were "degenerate" and needed to be destroyed. The country's youth were put into Nazi organizations, and the media were turned into a Nazi propaganda instrument.

Labor camps for criminals and other undesirables were set up and filled quickly. Simultaneously, the Jewish population was subjected to more and more restrictions, such as bans from certain professions. Measures against the Jews worsened with the Nuremberg Laws of 1935, which declared, among other things, that Jews were no longer German citizens and that sexual relations between Jews and the supposedly racially pure Germans were illegal. During the terrifying night of November 9, 1938, which came to be known as the Night of Shattered Glass, Nazis burned synagogues, vandalized Jewish shops all across the country, and lynched Jewish people. But the worst was reserved for those Jews who did not flee Germany in response to the growing injustice. At the Wannsee Conference in 1942, the Nazi leadership agreed upon the complete destruction of "European Jewry." Millions of Jewish people and other targeted groups were deported to concentration camps and systematically murdered.

The war Hitler imposed on the world started with his annexation of German-speaking parts of Czechoslovakia and all of Austria. Soon thereafter he attacked first Poland and then numerous other countries. Paris, Warsaw, and large parts of Russia became German territories. London was the subject of German bombing raids. When the progress into Russia finally slowed and the other Allied countries prepared for their invasion in the West, Hitler's fanaticism and his powerful position within the army blocked the way to early surrender. Over one hundred thousand German soldiers died in the Battle of Stalingrad alone, yet Hitler still hoped to win the war. Not even the near total destruction of the medieval city of Dresden, and several other major German cities, dissuaded him from continuing to prosecute the war—even though it was clear to most of the country that the war was all but lost. Finally, Hitler committed suicide in his bunker in Berlin as Allied troops approached the capital, and the German surrender was issued by others after there was literally nothing left to lose.

Today, many decades later, Germans learn about all this at school. The failure of the Weimar democracy, the Holocaust, and Hitler's war crimes are the themes of extended discussions and analyses in all parts of society. Much has been done to deal with the humbling past. Nonetheless, it will be a long time before the German term the *Führer* ("leader") can be used again without evoking the image of Hitler the demagogue.

Chapter 1

Political and Social Conditions That Contributed to Hitler's Rise

1

The Versailles Treaty Opened the Door for Hitler

Michael A. Boden

After losing World War I, Germany had to agree to the Versailles treaty, which assigned to Germany blame for the war and included substantial demands for reparation. The settlement caused anger and resentment among the German population, Michael A. Boden argues, and did much to foster nationalist sentiments that Nazis were able to exploit. Boden is a history instructor at the U.S. Military Academy, West Point.

"A fearful and gloomy existence awaits us in the best of circumstances!" So wrote historian Friedrich Meinecke in October 1918 as he and his countrymen looked with great anxiety to the end of World War I. His statement summed up the collective sense of the entire German nation quite well. The conclusion of the conflict failed to bring about the establishment of a long-term peace. Of the treaties that comprised the Peace of Paris, the Treaty of Versailles in June 1919 brought with it several elements that antagonized and disconcerted Germany. By failing to conclude a peace in which all participating parties could agree, the victorious Allies ensured that the future of Europe would be filled with dissension about the harsh terms of the agreement.

The Treaty of Versailles, which the Allies concluded without any German representation, gave German lands

Michael A. Boden, "The Treaty of Versailles and Nazism," *History in Dispute, Vol. 4: World War II, 1939–1943*, edited by Dennis Showalter. Farmington Hills, MI: St. James Press, 2000. Copyright © 2000 by The Gale Group. Reproduced by permission.

outright to France, Belgium, Poland, and to the League of Nations to administer. The treaty removed all German colonies from Berlin's control, and did the same to much of Germany proper, including the Saarland and the Rhineland. The German Army was capped at one hundred thousand men, with severe constraints on research, development, and training. Finally, Article 231 of the treaty forced Germany to accept responsibility for causing the war and for all of the damage and destruction that occurred in Europe from its aggression. These incredibly harsh terms greatly alienated Germany from the new world order that the victors envisioned and indeed laid the foundation for the rise of radical political elements in Germany, of which Adolf Hitler's National Socialist German Workers' Party (Nazi Party) proved to be the most successful. As Thomas Mann, the great German novelist, wrote, "having been robbed, the Germans became a nation of robbers." German people greeted the conclusion of the Versailles treaty with shock and indignation. This immediate and antagonistic reaction had two important results: the rise of German nationalism and the beginning of an economic crisis that led to disenchantment. In the end, the harsh terms of Versailles led the German people to support the radical policies of Hitler and the Nazis.

The War Guilt Clause

The one element of the Treaty of Versailles that perhaps inspired these feelings of betrayal and angst was Article 231, the War Guilt Clause. That article forced Germany to accept not only the responsibility for the war, but also for the prewar posturing and diplomatic aggression that culminated in the world conflict. This notion particularly galled most Germans, who felt that they had suffered as much as any other people during the four years of fighting; certainly Germany bore no more guilt for the war than any other European power. They simply could not accept the argument that they had started the war. Upon hearing the terms of the treaty, Philipp Scheidemann, a Social Democratic leader not known for radical nationalism, exclaimed, "What hand will not wither that delivers us into such chains?" With this attitude prevailing among the moderate German statesmen, what could the reaction possibly be among the more conservative and bellicose?

German nationalism was a delicate topic from the end

of the war and was closely tied with the problems that arose within Germany regarding the questions of whose fault it was that Germany lost the war. With members of the conservative parties and military supporters blaming socialists and liberals for stabbing the German nation in the back, the Weimar Republic was established on rocky footing. The publication of the terms of Versailles hardly helped this unsettled genesis. Within Germany people tended to view the deliberations with at least a modicum of good faith, notwithstanding the fact that no German representative had been invited to the treaty conference. When the harsh nature of the terms was disclosed, it unleashed a flurry of anger in Germany, particularly against American president Woodrow Wilson.

Only Limited German Self-Determination

Germans took Wilson's call for self-determination for all peoples to include Germany, too. Many Germans believed that the Allies had betrayed them. Self-determination apparently applied only to those countries who had been opposed to Germany. Worse still, large amounts of territory were taken away from Germany, and even regions that remained part of Germany proper were placed under foreign administration, including Austria, the Saarland, and the Danzig Corridor. The formulation of a League of Nations, led by Great Britain and France and excluding Germany, further solidified this sense of betrayal. It did not help matters that the two European leaders of this new organization soon engaged in a diplomatic race to exert their own authority over Germany's former colonies. In German eyes, the League became nothing more than a tool of anti-German territorial enforcement. The German population began to feel that they now stood alone against an antagonistic world in the face of grave, and possibly fatal, threats to their national existence. Similar thought processes helped lead the country toward a policy of passive resistance in the Ruhr in 1923.

The Versailles treaty further stoked the embers of German nationalism by imparting an intense antagonism toward France and anything French. The hostility and enmity between Germany and France became particularly bitter, standing out among the former combatants of World War I. French leaders made no secret of the fact that they desired, first, a permanent peace and, second, a German nation that never again could dominate the Continent. The French did not appear to want a lull in hostilities or a resumption of a world with a balance of power; they wanted full power on the Continent. Subsequent events bore this fear out to Germany. Even some French leaders seemed to foresee the problems, as French marshal Ferdinand Foch remarked despondently and with disturbing foresight: "This is not peace, it is an armistice for twenty years."

The Reparation Payments

The Versailles treaty also drove Germany into the arms of Hitler and the Nazi Party through the stringent application of monetary reparation payments, as well as the arbitrary and high-handed way the Allies forced them upon Germany. The publishing of British economist John Maynard Keynes's *Economic Consequences of the Peace* (1919) publicly served notice that reparations would be a problematic issue from the outset. In this pamphlet, Keynes stated emphatically that Germany could not pay back the initial demands and that this would lead to global financial turmoil. While the accuracy of this argument can be debated, its impact on the people of Germany cannot. Keynes's thesis was emblematic of the German peoples' cry of unfair treatment. The monumental difficulties of making the payments provided a mental justification and legitimization of their belief that the victorious Allies punished them unfairly. As if it were a harbinger of things to come, the debate over reparations did not die down, as many on the Allied side had hoped it would following an ever-lengthening period of peace. On the contrary, all sides continued to debate the issue hotly for the next thirteen years until payments were discontinued in 1932 as a result of the Great Depression.

In the end, the harsh terms of Versailles led the German people to support the radical policies of Hitler and the Nazis.

While German representatives at least were invited to most of the deliberations on the reparation schedules, Allied leaders seldom paid much heed to their input. Unchanging factors in the Allied camp continued to alienate Germany in the diplomatic realm and also made clear to them that they would continue to be required to pay unconscionably high amounts in reparation. First, the French continued to insist that Germany pay for the physical damages of the war. In the French view, western-front warfare had been conducted chiefly on French soil. Flanders and Northeast France had been devastated by the war, and the victors did not believe it their own responsibility to pay for rebuilding. Second, while Great Britain and the United States were antagonistic toward French demands concerning payments, British leaders were unsuccessful in their efforts to persuade France to reduce their demands. Great Britain saw itself as one of the leaders in the postwar world and desired to reincorporate Germany into the community of nations. Only through such a reincorporation could a healthy global-economic system and structure be reestablished. The United States, for its part, had lapsed into a strong isolationist stance, where the actual damages paid by Germany to the European powers was of distant importance to American policy objectives. These objectives comprise the third constant: the United States insisted on repayment of its war debts owed by its allies, particularly France. American demands inspired European powers to pass on the burden to Germany through high reparation payments, deepening the German feeling of helplessness and resentment.

Hyperinflation and Radicalization

All of this early rancor reached a crucial point in 1923 with the Ruhr occupation and the German policy of passive resistance. The economy in Germany steadily grew worse, eventually devaluing to an exchange rate of 4.2 trillion marks to one U.S. dollar. When the *Rentenmark* (stablized mark based on land values) stabilized the economy during the final months of 1923, many Germans realized they had been wiped out or deeply affected by the repercussions of hyperinflation and the gradually eroding economic situation since the war years. Those Germans who had worked hard all of their lives and had earned enough money to invest or save found their efforts nullified in a single blow. Labor unions found it difficult to protect the jobs of their members and the movement lost much of its power and influence built up in the previous fifty years. Many of the disillusioned would become attracted to new, more radical political parties. In the words of Gordon Craig, in *Germany, 1866–1945* (1978), "Among those groups who had been actually or psychologically expropriated, the resentment was lasting and was reflected in political attitudes hostile to democracy." The Nazi Party benefited greatly from these feelings.

Those Germans who had worked hard all of their lives and had earned enough money to invest or save found their efforts nullified in a single blow.

The reparation debate did not go away. Ongoing debates led first to the Dawes Plan in August of 1924, then to the Young Plan in 1929, then, after the stock-market crash of 1929, to the temporary moratorium on payments in 1931. Finally, the Allies completely terminated all payments in 1932 at the Lausanne Conference (16 June–9 July). The debate continued to fuel acrimonious feelings in Germany, as Germans maintained that they had been swindled even as the French insisted that somehow they had failed to receive their due. The German-French enmity deepened over the reparation debates, as the two countries constantly contended throughout the 1920s over the amount and schedule of German reparation payments, figures the French always seemed to want to increase. The almost gleeful French and Belgian "invasion" of the Ruhr in January 1923 and imposition of foreign troops on Germany that followed surprised few, and it led to the German policy of passive resistance, an important outlet for the expression of German spirit. That tactic also caused two significant events that greatly facilitated the rise of Hitler: the climax of hyperinflation and the fall of Gustav Stresemann as chancellor.

There was no easy solution or smooth transition to a post-reparation world, and the debate left lasting scars on the German psyche. The coming of the Great Depression and the ending of reparation payments ended the direct impact of the Versailles treaty on the future of Germany. Its indirect and long-term effects, however, had serious consequences. The feeling of hopelessness and the singular stance against the rest of the free world that Germans felt led to a surge in German nationalism. The failure and unwillingness of the victors to consider a modification of the treaty over the ensuing decade and a half turned this nationalism into the driving force behind new German conceptions of nation and purpose. Economic hardships continually and disdainfully imposed by the Allies on a defeated power had effects far beyond its negative impact on the financial stability of Germany, for the instability it bred helped to ignite the radical party politics, in many cases precisely in those social groups most likely to be antiradical. The Treaty of Versailles, and the many ill feelings it fostered, turned many German citizens to the radical politics of Hitler and the Nazi Party.

2

The Nazis Benefited from the Problems of the Weimar Republic

Michael Burleigh

During the Weimar democracy, the first in Germany's history, crucial problems helped propel the Nazis to power. In particular, Michael Burleigh argues, the Great Depression, which struck in 1929, led to unemployment rates of over 30 percent and fostered despair and desperation in both the city and countryside. In such a volatile society, according to Burleigh, political extremists such as the Nazis found it easy to win supporters because they offered the promise of bold and swift change. On a practical level, the Nazis offered a bed and a bowl of soup to jobless young men, thereby swelling their membership. Burleigh is a research professor at Cardiff University in Great Britain. The piece is taken from his award-winning book *The Third Reich: A New History*.

Germany's National Assembly, consisting of delegates elected in mid-January 1919, convened in the small Thuringian town of Weimar to draft and approve a republican constitution, while the government scrutinised Allied peace terms. The two things were connected, in that the choice of meeting place was designed to show the Allies that a new Germany, informed by the town of [writer Johann Wolfgang von] Goethe, had come into being.

The fundaments of the constitution were established before the Assembly met: there was to be a democratic, fed-

Michael Burleigh, *The Third Reich: A New History*. London: Macmillan, 2000.
Copyright © 2000 by Michael Burleigh. Reproduced by permission of Macmillan, London and Basingstoke.

eral republic based on the dualism of presidency and parliament. Earlier agreements among political, industrial and military leaders set the limits on what was thought possible, and the constitution effectively enshrined the compromises of the first non-violent phase of Germany's revolution. On 11 February the Assembly elected [Friedrich] Ebert president, who in turn called on Philipp Scheidemann to form a government based on a coalition of Majority Social Democrats, the Catholic Centre Party and the liberal German Democratic Party, parties which had a wartime track-record of co-operation and which, in January, had obtained a mandate consisting of over 76 per cent of votes cast. Left-liberal lawyers assumed the main burden of drafting the constitution, although the influence of representatives of the Churches and the federal states made themselves felt for better or for worse. There were sticking points over the national flag, the status of religious education and the rights of the constituent regional states, but these constitutional deliberations were concluded remarkably swiftly between February and August 1919.

Rejection of the Versailles treaty was common across the Weimar political spectrum.

Since the liberal drafters of the constitution were historically wary of overweening parliamentary powers, the constitution combined an elected presidency, which was granted emergency powers, with an elected parliament for which all persons over twenty could vote. The electoral cycle for parliament was four years, and seven years for the presidency. The presidency was designed to be a largely honorary figurehead position, filling the vacuum left by Germany's exiled monarch, although the occupants (only the second of whom, [Paul von] Hindenburg, was popularly elected) showed few signs of charismatic appeal. Apart from the obligation to perform tasks which normally befall heads of state, the president had the power to dissolve parliament, to nominate as chancellors persons either enjoying or likely to enjoy the support of a parliamentary majority (which was by no means a foregone conclusion), and, under Article 48, to issue emergency legislation and to deploy the armed forces to restore order. This last stipulation was ominously vague. Ebert availed himself 136 times of emergency decrees, many of a very technical nature and mostly during the crises that arose in 1923, while Hindenburg, his successor, issued none between 1925 and 1930, and rescinded eight of Ebert's. At the time few thought of the potential misuse of this last power; and Weimar's constitution can hardly be held responsible alone for the advent of a racist, totalitarian dictatorship. . . .

Prolonging the War

However reasonable the Allied case for Germany's obligation to provide restitution for material damage and loss of shipping, and to pay pensions for veterans, widows and orphans, the political message seemed to be that the Versailles treaty [that ended World War I] was prolonging the war by economic means. For, beyond a desire to neutralise Germany's military might, there seemed to be an intention to disable permanently the economic power underpinning it, regardless of transformed domestic political circumstances, and despite the deleterious economic and psychological consequences for the stability of the Weimar Republic. All these fears, some of them justified, coupled with the Allies' latent threat of armed intervention to enforce the treaty's terms, contributed to the view that Germany after 1918 was engaged in a sort of cold war.

Superficially speaking, Versailles created unanimity among Germans. But this overworked paradox was more apparent than real. Moderate opponents of the treaty opted for negotiation to obtain revised terms, the line pursued ineptly or shrewdly by successive Weimar chancellors and their foreign ministers from Joseph Wirth via Gustav Stresemann to Heinrich Brüning, but diehard opponents of the Republic convinced themselves that the 'November criminals', as they dubbed the republicans who had toppled the Kaiser [Kaiser Wilhelm II, who reigned from 1888 to 1918] and surrendered to the Allies, were responsible for Germany's defeat and this shamefully onerous peace treaty. Once people had worked themselves into a lather, reality counted for nothing. No matter how ingeniously a great statesman such as Stresemann employed reconciliation and an ideology of Europeanism to dismantle the Versailles framework, he could never satisfy appetites whetted since the 1880s by visions of Germany's obtaining both a continental and an overseas empire at one fell swoop, which would redress the grievance Germany felt towards more established colonial powers. The Republic's foreign policy inevitably fell short of such insatiable expectations, as had also happened during the Wilhelmine empire, whose foreign policy had never been quite strident enough for sections of nationalist opinion. . . .

Rejection of the Versailles treaty was common across the Weimar political spectrum, including the Communists, who regarded it as part of a wider intra-imperialist plot. There was no distinctive political advantage in opposing it. Many of the most transparently coercive features of the settlement—such as military inspectorates, occupied zones and reparations—had largely unravelled before Nazism became a mass political movement, in a Europe which was by no means universally unsympathetic to Germany's legitimate grievances.

Obligation and Order Came Before Individual Rights

However, the widely acknowledged iniquities of the Versailles treaty were elided by many right-wing Germans with a broader charge of treason against the alleged 'November criminals', which was both inaccurate and preposterous. *Ad hominem* libels and political terrorism which supported and furthered these false accusations were avowedly intended to undermine the newly democratic order. This order was also traduced by the intellectual right as an alien, mechanical, Westernised import, an aberration from Germany's allegedly authoritarian national tradition which had recently transformed myriad sleepy principalities into a great European power. This line simply ignored the vibrant party political culture that had marked the Wilhelmine empire. The fictive 'civic truce', which some Germans claimed had characterised German society during the war, mutated into an imagined 'national community' transcending class conflict, where obligation and order superseded Western liberal notions of individual rights. Of course, in other parts of German life, among Catholics and socialists, there were alternative versions of 'national community'—based on Christian principles, loyalty to the Republic and a desire for social justice—which deserve not to be overlooked. But the unreconciled right was more interested in going forward boldly into the future in search of an imaginary past. Accuracy, fair play and respect for either persons or institutions were not high priorities in its enraged milieu, and their chorus was joined, from the far left, by venomous assaults against the alleged betrayers of the socialist revolution and snide demimondiste attacks on putative German national characteristics which irritated plain provincial people. The so-called intelligentsia which took this line scorned the dull and worthy politicians of the day, and they mocked the armed forces and their fellow countrymen in general, whose stolid values and virtues they despised, just as their right-wing counterparts fulminated against 'the masses' and Germany's new inorganic Weimar political 'system', a word well chosen for insinuating something inauthentically alien and mechanical. . . .

The Payment of Reparations

Allied reparations demands occasioned Weimar Germany's next bout of crises. In April 1921 an Allied commission presented the bill. It totalled 132 billion gold Marks or about US$30 billion. This was the scaled-down figure, for only British and American pressure had stymied France's demands for 269 billion Marks. Chancellor Joseph Wirth opted for tactical compliance, if only to demonstrate Germany's incapacity to pay. For the Allies, having imposed reparations on Germany, unhelpfully passed the business of deciding how to raise the money on to the Germans themselves to avoid the costs of military occupation. France threatened to extend the occupation, but this was a bluff waiting to be called, especially since such influential Englishmen as the economist John Maynard Keynes were by no means unsympathetic to equally weighty German descriptions of Germany's alleged plight.

Production slowed as workers trundled carts laden with a day's pay to the banks, and shops shut as the owners ceased to be able to purchase new stock with yesterday's takings.

The payment arrangements meant that reparations to the Allies had to compete with the German government's desire to purchase social peace by postponing the stabilisation of the economy, at a time when the Allies were experiencing deflation and high unemployment. . . .

When over Christmas and New Year 1922–3 Germany twice defaulted on her reparations obligations, seventy thousand French and Belgian troops occupied the Ruhr [Valley, a highly industrialized region], ostensibly to protect engineers seizing telegraph poles and timber, but really to secure the economic edge that France and Belgium had failed to acquire under the Versailles treaty. The new centre-right cabinet of the Hamburg businessman Wilhelm Cuno, whom Ebert had appointed to make an impression of seriousness on the Allies, ironically endorsed a campaign of passive resistance among the Ruhr's inhabitants, having undertaken no advanced planning or stockpiling for this eventuality. Passive resistance in the Ruhr led to the French authorities expelling or imprisoning recalcitrants. To be precise, about 46,200 civil servants, railwaymen and police were directly affected, together with a hundred thousand of their relatives. Sporadic sabotage and low-level acts of terrorism, which according to some exponents were explicitly modelled on the corrosive acts of Irish Republican terrorism against the British, were countered robustly with shootings, hostage-taking and collective fines. Having already blotted their copybooks by knocking German civilians off the pavements, the occupying forces compounded their errors by aggressive house searches, and identity checks, and summary executions. Courts martial created nationalist martyrs, notoriously Albert Leo Schlageter, who was shot in 1923 by the French occupation authorities. . . .

The Consequences of the Ruhr Occupation

The economic consequences of the Allies' occupation of the Ruhr in 1923 were catastrophic. The German government used deficit spending to subsidise workers summarily dismissed from their posts while purchasing coal from Britain. The cessation of deliveries of raw materials from the Ruhr resulted in waves of cutbacks in production and layoffs elsewhere. Unemployment rose from 2 to 23 per cent. Tax revenue declined to the point where by October 1923 it covered a mere 1 per cent of total government expenditure. The volume of money circulating in Germany grew astronomically, by the autumn flowing in improbable denominations from nearly two thousand presses operating around the clock. A banknote-printers' bill appeared as 32776899763734490417 Marks and 5 pfennige in Reichsbank accounts. Banks had to hire more clerical workers to calculate these lengthening digits. Production slowed as workers trundled carts laden with a day's pay to the banks, and shops shut as the owners ceased to be able to purchase new stock with yesterday's takings. In a chapter entitled 'The Death of Money', Konrad Heiden tells the following story:

> A man who thought he had a small fortune in the bank might receive a letter from the directors: 'The bank deeply regrets that it can no longer administer your deposit of sixty-eight thousand marks, since the costs are out of all proportion to the capital. We are therefore taking the liberty of returning your capital. Since we have no bank-notes in small enough denominations at our disposal, we have rounded out the sum to one million marks. Enclosure: one 1,000,000-mark bill'. A cancelled stamp for five million marks adorned the envelope.

A barter economy developed and the prudent middle classes began selling their most cherished possessions, although there were only so many Steinway pianos a peasant house could accommodate. Books were devoted to the moral inversions inflation caused.

Prostitution and Suicide

The perception grew that, as in wartime, the scum rose to the top. Decent hardworking people thought they were being exploited by amoral spivs, flashing their ill-gotten gains in nightclubs and restaurants, while doctors, lawyers and students had to resort to manual labour or soup kitchens. There was an unappetising type abroad in the land:

> Connoisseurs of the time should wander one evening through the parlours and fancy eating establishments—everywhere, in every lousy corner you will smack up against the same plump face of the potbellied profiteers of war and peace.

According to the author of this essay, entitled 'Berlin is becoming a whore', the hundred thousand prostitutes who allegedly serviced Berlin were no longer servants who had been dismissed after an upstairs–downstairs liaison, but nice middle-class girls:

A university professor earns less than a streetcar conductor, but the scholar's daughter was used to wearing silk stockings. It is no accident that the nude dancer Celly de Rheidt is the wife of a former Prussian officer. Thousands of bourgeois families are now being forced, if they want to live uprightly on their budget, to leave their six room apartments and adopt a vegetarian diet. This impoverishment of the bourgeoisie is necessarily bound up with women accustomed to luxury turning into whores. . . . The impoverished noblewoman becomes a bar maid; the discharged naval officer makes films; the daughter of the provincial judge cannot expect her father to make her a present of her winter clothes.

Differentials between earnings were erased, leading to an acute sense of social declassification, which was soon epitomised by a middle-class Militant League of Beggars. People suffering from clinical malnutrition, and unable to afford adequate food or medicine, were susceptible to tuberculosis or rickets. Although the 'Mark is a Mark' policy was endorsed by the courts and enabled farmers and mortgagees to pay off their creditors, pensioners, savers and elderly people living off modest rental incomes were plunged into poverty and insecurity. Sometimes their only escape from indignity was through suicide. . . .

The Great Depression

The onset of the 1929 world economic Depression immeasurably radicalised the political climate in Germany. . . . The Depression created an atmosphere of despair and led to a corresponding resort to desperate solutions. Germany literally became unsafe as paramilitary armies (although that term dignifies squalid thuggery) contested each other on the nation's streets. . . . Violence bred further violence, with the leader of the largest paramilitary army of all posing as a defender of law and order, even as he exculpated the murders committed by his own followers. The Nazis' dual-track strategy of the ballot box and the gun, boot or fist immeasurably complicated the responses of the authorities to them.

Connections between economic distress and political extremism were not straightforward. Chronic unemployment was as likely to lead to a day in bed as to seeking to overthrow the Weimar constitution. And the unemployed had minds of their own, when others—notably Communists and Nazis—cynically tried to exploit their plight for political purposes.

The number of registered unemployed rose from 1.6 million in October 1929 to 6.12 million in February 1932. Since these figures did not include the 'invisible' unregistered unemployed, the 1932 figure can be increased to a minimum of 7.6 million, perhaps a million or so more. Thirty-three per cent of the workforce were without jobs. Taking into account dependants, perhaps twenty-three million people were affected by unemployment. Unemployment of this magnitude overstretched an insurance system designed to cope with only eight hundred thousand jobless people. . . .

Mass Unemployment

It is perhaps salutary to remind ourselves what unemployment involved: in places where it was chronic and virtually total, people suffered a gradual loss of self-worth, a shrinking of mental horizons, a diminution of skills and often a collapse of the will to work. This last became one justification for imposing compulsory labour, such as dredging canals and ditches or mowing verges. Local governments also used compulsory labour to offload the burden of unemployment back on federal government, claiming that the work requalified the unemployed for national insurance.

Extremist parties cynically attempted to exploit people's misery.

The unemployed spent their days reading newspapers, smoking, standing in meal queues, squabbling at benefit offices or loitering aimlessly in parks and on street corners. Men tried to keep warm in waiting rooms and fed themselves by scavenging in dustbins. Their clothing became frayed and threadbare, the soles of their shoes worn, making it harder to find jobs since appearances counted. Others held signs or carried placards advertising their desire to work. Many became apathetic and resigned to being unemployed. Others grew desperate. By 1932, the German suicide rate stood at 260 per million (as against 85 in Britain and 133 in the United States). Since women were paid less than men, they found it easier to get jobs and worked while their husbands and sons brooded at home, an inversion of the gender roles normal at the time that made for domestic fractiousness. Hopelessness spread to children, who absorbed their parents' despair. Malnourished and fatigued—there was a new fashion for cheap child labour—they could not concentrate at school. In big cities, some teenagers went around in anti-social packs—the 'Wild cliques', numbering fourteen thousand in Berlin alone, led by 'clique bulls' surrounded by simpering 'clique cows'. There was a rise in juvenile crime, prostitution, vagrancy and vandalism, and also in the population in remand homes and the juvenile wings of prisons.

Soup Kitchens and Homelessness

Since unemployment was concentrated in certain regions—at its highest in the fifty industrial cities and lowest in Germany's less industrialised south—some four hundred thousand people took to the roads in search of work, which stimulated further anxieties about tramps and vagrants. Those dependent on meagre local benefits lived on bread and potatoes or whatever they could beg or steal, with heating fuel scratched off the slagheaps. People stood in line for the unappetising fare of soup kitchens. There was a shocking increase in cases of impetigo, rickets and pulmonary illnesses. As the proportion of income spent on housing rose from 10 to 50 per cent, the number of evictions mounted, and many unemployed workers moved to squatter settlements in the suburbs. Former industrial workers went back to being subsistence gatherers and farmers, stealing or scratching food from allotments. An enterprising few tried to make a go of it by selling beer, fruit or razor blades on street corners. This vicious circle of self-help by the unemployed undercut small businesses, already suffering from a drop in demand. And the poverty of urban workers affected the countryside. Livestock farmers in Schleswig-Holstein borrowed money to purchase calves in spring, which after being fattened throughout the summer were slaughtered and sold in Altona, Hamburg, Kiel and Lübeck in the autumn to liquidate their debts. Since the unemployed could barely afford bread and potatoes, this spelled ruin for many livestock farmers.

Germans who did have jobs faced wage cuts—some introduced through direct appeals to the workforce over the heads of the union representatives—shortened work hours, or compulsory alternation with the unemployed. In some plants, for example at I.G. Farben, chemists and engineers over fifty-five years of age were let go and younger men kept a form of industrial triage. The workers' trust in their union representatives declined, as the latter clung to unrealistic wage levels even if this meant a factory would close down. Depression both reinforced and undermined solidarities. In some plants, management received anonymous denunciations of idling union officials: 'Out with the trades union bosses, the party is over here.' War veterans wanted the 'red cowards' who 'had never seen trenches, dirt, lice and hardship or heard the fire of three thousand cannon' first out of the factory doors.

The Nazis Exploit the Misery

Mass unemployment contributed to political extremism in complex ways. That many unemployed people were extremely bitter is unsurprising, but their bitterness was expressed in forms often only tangentially related to what those seeking to exploit their distress envisaged. Bailiffs who planned evictions were sometimes scared off by organised mobs, while municipal benefits offices became extremely charged environments, where the staff exasperated the unemployed by insensitive probing into their affairs, the result being flying chairs and inkwells and the arrival of the police, who were sometimes more sympathetic to the unemployed. Extremist parties cynically attempted to exploit people's misery. In Berlin, [Nazi Joseph] Goebbels' *Der Angriff* [The Attack] published lists of suicides, along with digs at the initial promises of the Republic: 'He was no longer able to bear the good fortune of this life in beauty and dignity.' The SA [Nazi Storm Troopers] opened up hostels where its unemployed members were sure of a bed and a square meal, arrangements that gave the Nazis a pool of toughs and, when this access to free soup was extended to the unemployed, advertised their brand of real, existing socialism. But the Nazis were only indirect political beneficiaries of unemployment. Middle-class reactions to unemployment alternated between compassion and fear. The former took the form of free food and cheap fuel. The latter was a compound in most of the responses to the crisis discussed here, such as rising juvenile crime, but also in the middle-class accusations that the unemployed were workshy and the visceral anxiety that unemployment might trigger bankruptcies. Finally, since about 30 per cent of the unemployed showed a clear sympathy for the Communists, the increase in their vote and the heightening of their anti-capitalist rhetoric helped to propel other anxious voters towards the Nazis.

3

Hitler Gained Power by Legal Means

H.W. Koch

Hitler did not seize control in Germany by force or deception. Rather, he gained power legally, taking advantage of weaknesses in the Weimar Constitution and the seeming reluctance of members of the Reichstag to dispute his interpretation of that document.

So argues historian H.W. Koch, who writes that Hitler's appointment as chancellor in 1933 was constitutional, as were the copious emergency decrees he would soon thereafter enact. For example, with civil unrest threatening the peace, Hitler used Article 48 of the constitution as the basis for a decree that all public assemblies be subject to prior police approval. Hitler's call for passage of the Enabling Law and its subsequent enactment by Reichstag members led directly—and legally—to the dissolution of parliament and the führer's accession to absolute power.

Hitler detested the legal profession. Lawyers, legal experts and ministerial bureaucrats—and more often than not they were identical—were a nightmare for Hitler; he intuitively felt that they acted as a brake on his more fantastic plans. On the other hand, he was a great admirer of Frederick the Great's *Landrat* administration, all of whom were fully trained in the law. No doubt part of Hitler's dislike of the legal profession originated during the Weimar Republic when, for instance, it was possible in Berlin for criminal gangs to establish their headquarters in restaurants

H.W. Koch, *In the Name of the Volk: Political Justice in Hitler's Germany*. London: I.B. Tauris & Company, Ltd., 1989. Copyright © 1989 by H.W. Koch. Reproduced by permission of the publisher.

between the Alexanderplatz and Friedrichshain, where they held their annual balls, undisturbed by the police and the judiciary, the executive condemned to inaction because of legal technicalities.

Hitler's One Respected Jurist

Hitler could explode into paroxysms of hate against the judiciary when he came across light sentences against traitors and the murderers of women and children and this was one reason why, for instance, Fritz Lang's film 'M', in which Peter Lorre played a demented child murderer, was immediately withdrawn from circulation in 1933. Sometimes he accused the judiciary of pettiness, for example when a case came to his ears in which the will of an elderly woman was declared invalid who, because of her infirmity, could no longer sign the will and instead had her name typed in. The only jurist he really respected was Dr Heinrich Lammers, since 1922 Ministerial Counsellor in the Ministry of the Interior and from 1933 to 1945 Chief of the Reich Chancellery, first as Secretary of State and then as Reich Minister. In Hitler's view, Lammers knew that his task was to produce legal foundations for measures he judged necessary in the interest of state; he did not confuse legal abstractions with practical life. In Hitler's eyes, Lammers had not lost his sound common sense in spite of his doctorate in law, which of course in practice meant that Lammers was not troubled by any scruples when weaving veils of legality over manifestly illegal acts.

The Weimar Constitution contained nothing which made it illegal to change the Constitution or even abolish it, provided there was the necessary two-thirds majority in the Reichstag.

On one occasion Hitler stated that [Nazi foreign minister Joachim von] Ribbentrop was quite right in urging the reorganization of the German Foreign Service, because every German Foreign Office member active abroad represented the Reich. If he made an error or simply a bad impression, then this would damage the whole of the Reich. A civil servant of the judiciary, however, could be completely mad and cause heaven knows what nonsense, and no cock would crow after him, except when the Reich suffered an obvious irreparable damage. Hitler summed up his general opinion on the legal profession: they were as international as criminals, but not half as clever.

The Legality of Hitler's Chancellorship

Nevertheless, Hitler was always anxious to have his actions legally secured. The Weimar Constitution contained nothing which made it illegal to change the Constitution or even abolish it, provided there was the necessary two-thirds majority in the Reichstag [parliament]. The Weimar Constitution also contained elements of direct democracy such as the referendum and the plebiscite, and the possibility of unlimited constitutional change by way of legislation according to Article 76. Hence Hitler's appointment as Chancellor was well within the framework of the Constitution and in fact was rather more constitutional than any of the governments that had come and gone since the break-up of the Great Coalition of 1930. According to the letter of the Constitution, Hitler's appointment meant a return of government into normal parliamentary channels, i.e. as outlined in Articles 54 and 32 of the Constitution, which stated that the Chancellor and his ministers required the confidence of the Reichstag to conduct their office. That confidence was expressed by the majority vote of the Reichstag. Up to that point everything was normal; the abnormal situation arose only after 23 March 1933 when Hitler succeeded in having his Enabling Bill enacted as law.

The Emergency Decrees

In the meantime, however, there were to be new elections: the Reichstag was dissolved on 1 February 1933. Given the civil war climate in which the two presidential and two Reichstag elections of 1932 were carried out, it was not unnatural that emergency decrees were introduced in order to curb and to contain excesses, a precedent being [General Wilhelm] Groener's legislation of 1932—revoked by [Chancellor Franz von] Papen later in the year—prohibiting the NSDAP's [National Socialist Democratic Workers' Party—the Nazis] paramilitary formations. In his role as Deputy Commissar for Prussia, [Hermann] Göring had already on 30 January and again on 2 February introduced a decree prohibiting Communist public demonstrations. On 4 February followed national emergency legislation based on Article 48 of the Constitution which subjected all public assemblies to prior police approval and prohibited all assemblies in the open air which could pose a potential threat to public order and security. The freedom of the press was constrained and a ban was placed on publications 'whose content is likely to endanger public security and order.'

The National Socialists did not expect to hold to power uncontested and anticipated some sort of left-wing uprising. They expected that they would be called upon to fight it out in the streets. Because in Prussia the police force had over the past thirteen years been heavily infiltrated by Social Democrats, Göring took the SA and SS [Nazi 'Storm Troopers' and 'Security Squadron,' respectively] as an 'auxiliary force' into the Prussian police; it was inevitable that in the process of their 'executive duties' some old scores were settled. However, the point of culmination was reached when the Dutchman Marinus van der Lubbe set fire to the Reichstag [building], destroying its entire interior. The subsequent emergency legislation enacted on 28 February 1933, also based on Article 48 of the Constitution, was the product of *ad hoc* improvisation, and not the result of long-term planning.

In other words, the parties of the Weimar Republic were not deceitfully removed or even smashed; they removed themselves.

Among Hitler and his entourage the conviction was firm that the Reichstag fire was the signal for a Communist uprising or at least a general strike. The emergency legislation suspended all the basic rights of the Constitution and was supplemented on 21 March 1933 by a law directed against 'treacherous attacks against the Government of the National Revolution'. . . . Although the Communist uprising never materialized, this legislation remained in force until the end of the Third Reich.

In spite of this, the KPD [Communist Party of Germany] was not officially prohibited until June 1933, although such a course was advocated by [Alfred] Hugenberg in cabinet prior to the Reichstag fire but opposed by Hitler.

Though numerous Communists were arrested, many of them put in improvised SA concentration camps, they were still allowed to participate in the election held on 5 March 1933. For the NSDAP the election proved a disappointment. It did not gain its hoped-for absolute majority but received 43.9 per cent of all the votes. Thanks only to its allies in the German National People's Party (DNVP) could the NSDAP state that 56 per cent of the German population supported the 'Government of the National Revolution'.

The Enabling Bill

The election results nonetheless offered the party a position of strength. At the first meeting of the Reichstag, Hitler introduced his Enabling Bill, which was to give him unlimited powers for the 'Recovery of Germany' for a period of four years. Hitler's aim was to gain unlimited power in Germany. He had said so often enough. 'We National Socialists,' he proclaimed, 'have never asserted ourselves representatives of the democratic point of view, but have openly declared that we take recourse to democratic means only to win power and that after our seizure of power we shall decline without any hesitation to afford to our opponents all those means which were put at our disposal in times of opposition. And in the

Hitler is sworn in as chancellor on January 30, 1933.

same year he declared: '. . . for us parliament is not an end in itself, but a means to an end. In principle we are not a parliamentary party, that would contradict our entire concept. Under duress we are a parliamentary party and what forces us to use such means is the Constitution.'

Hitler was quite aware that over the long term Article 48 of the Constitution would be entirely inadequate. What Hitler needed was a blank cheque. Only Article 76 of the Weimar Constitution could provide him with that. Article 76 stipulated that the Constitution could only be changed by way of legislation, and any such change required the assent of two-thirds of the quorum of Reichstag deputies, the quorum itself being two-thirds of the total number of Reichstag deputies. In the event, the Social Democrats alone voted against it; even the full Communist presence would have made no difference.

All Reichstag members who voted, even those not belonging to the NSDAP, knew that Hitler would break with the parliamentary system. They also knew what the Enabling Bill, called The Law for the Recovery of People and Reich from Suffering, which was released the following day, meant. Article 1 stated bluntly: 'Notwithstanding the procedure laid down in the Reich Constitution laws may be passed by the Reich government.' The principle of the separation of powers was blatantly broken, the opinion of the Reichstag ignored, and those who were to be ignored sanctioned this action. Article 2 stated that laws enacted under Article 1 might also deviate from the Constitution. In this way the Executive gained full powers over the Legislature and all by constitutional means.

Parliament's Enactment of the Enabling Bill

Much has been said and written about the intimidation of Reichstag deputies, about the alleged atmosphere of terror. Even if these allegations are true, the question remains as to why the SPD [Social Democratic Party] voted *en bloc* against the Enabling Bill while 82 per cent of Germany's full-time parliamentarians endowed Hitler with powers about the purpose and use of which there could be no doubt. Hitler was quite forthright and honest in his speech advocating the acceptance of the law. As regards Germany's legal system he said: 'The security of tenure of the judges on the one side must correspond on the other with an elasticity for the benefit of the community when reaching judgements. The centre of legal concern is not the individual but the Volk [people].' He continued:

> It would contradict the spirit of the National Revolution and not suffice for the intended purpose if to enact its measures the government had for each ease to request the agreement of the Reichstag. The government is not motivated by the intention of abolishing the Reichstag as such. On the contrary it reserves for itself the right to inform the Reichstag from time to time about its measures. . . . Since the government as such has a clear majority, the number of cases in which it has to take recourse to this law is in itself a limited one. All the more, however, the government of the National Revolution insists upon passing this law. In any case it prefers a clear decision. It offers the parties the possibility of peace and quiet and from that a way forward towards understanding in the future, but it is equally as decided and ready to accept the confirmation of rejection and thus the proclamation of resistance. May you now, my honourable deputies *(meine Herren Abgeordneten)*, make your own decision—peace or war!

This was clear enough; if more clarification was needed, SPD deputy Otto Wels in his speech defending his party's attitude pointed to all the implications of the bill. After that no deputy could maintain that his eyes had not been opened. Wels stated that the government had indeed obtained a clear majority in the elections but with the Enabling Bill the National Socialists intended nothing other than to take the final step in the direction of the dissolution of parliamentary democracy in Germany. For this purpose his party and the parliamentary part of the SPD could not be won over.

In other words, the parties of the Weimar Republic were not deceitfully removed or even smashed; they removed themselves. Hjalmar Schacht, Hitler's economic minister and president of the Reichsbank until 1938, remarked that the democratic parties unnecessarily relinquished their parliamentary influence, 'an act of political self-emasculation unknown in the history of modern democracy.' The parties themselves had put the Constitution out of operation on those issues decisive for a democratic structure. They had thus voluntary voted for their own dissolution.

Death of the Constitution

Weimar did not die because of its enemies, but because it possessed no genuine friends, not even among the Socialists. It did not have parties that unreservedly supported the state, only pall bearers that carried the coffin. Its trenchant left-wing critics, as the writer Kurt Tucholsky himself admitted shortly thereafter, lacked any sense of the boundaries between change and destruction. The Republic was managed by parties whose democratic loyalty was limited to their own party programme, and on occasion not even that. What the acceptance of the Enabling Bill proves is that the parties of the Weimar Republic were almost at one in their opinion that the liberal system on whose existence their own continuance depended, contained no possibilities for any political life in the future. The last act had ended, the curtains were drawn. Hitler kept his promise in his fashion; he did not abolish the Reichstag as such, but merely changed its composition to form an acclamatory assembly of the NSDAP which from time to time was called together to be informed about 'the measures of the government'. He even had the Enabling Law renewed, twice before the war, and once during it.

But even before the Enabling Bill was passed, the process of 'coordination' *(Gleichschaltung)* [Hitler's system of gaining total control over society]—institutional, political and psychological—had begun throughout Germany. The *Lands* were 'coordinated' into the Reich, each under a *Reichsstatthalter*, an official acting on behalf of central government. Despite this centralization of power, Hitler still expressed himself in favour of some degree of decentralization, and allowed his Gauleiters [local Nazi leaders] considerable freedom of operation. The Third Reich, far from being a firm monolith, was very much a polycratic structure, in which, however, Hitler had the last say. By July 1933 all political parties other than the NSDAP had disappeared. All this had become possible because of the Reichstag's action.

4

Ordinary People Contributed to Nazi Control

Robert Gellately

In the following article, Robert Gellately argues that ordinary Germans contributed to Hitler's terror system by reporting their fellow citizens to the Gestapo, the German secret police. Examples of acts reported include statements or remarks critical of Hitler and contact with Jewish Germans. Sometimes the motives for reporting someone were as simple as personal grudges against family members or disagreements with business partners. Consequently, it is argued, the allegations were often false. According to the author the Gestapo followed up on even patently questionable allegations, resulting in dreadful cross-examinations or even death in a concentration camp. Such denunciations by ordinary citizens, Gellately claims, helped the Nazis to socially isolate the undesired and were a crucial part of the Nazi power structure. Gellately is Professor and Strassler Family Chair for the Study of Holocaust History, Department of History, Clark University in Worcester, Massachusetts.

The legal façade surrounding the 'seizure of power' no doubt paid dividends in that many law-abiding citizens, out of respect for the legal norms, simply complied and co-operated with the new regime. Because the takeover was not patently illegal, many could choose to ignore its revolutionary character, especially after the radicals were subdued following the purge in June 1934. The stoic accep-

Robert Gellately, *The Gestapo and German Society: Enforcing Racial Policy: 1933–1945*. Oxford: Clarendon Press, 1990. Copyright © 1990 by Robert Gellately. Reproduced by permission of Oxford at the Clarendon Press.

tance, however, seems to have yielded to more positive attitudes. Hans Bernd Gisevius, a member of the Gestapo [the Nazi secret police] in 1933, later recalled that there was a new mood and a widespread (though far from unanimous) positive disposition towards the regime, especially in the efforts to put down the supposed Communist threat. What struck him most forcefully was what he called 'individual *Gleichschaltung* [co-ordination]', by which he meant a kind of willing self-integration into the new system.

The terror system had both a formal side—embracing the whole range of institutional arrangements—and an informal side that worked in tandem with those arrangements. Much less has been written about the 'informal' politics in the Nazi dictatorship, but there is much evidence to suggest that existing informal power-structures underwent adjustments as many people began to bring their attitudes on all kinds of issues into line. People may have experienced anxieties, but there were other positive factors at work. [Historian] Golo Mann remarked that even the massive force and brutality of the Nazi 'seizure of power' were to a considerable extent overlooked: 'it was the feeling that Hitler was historically right which made a large part of the nation ignore the horrors of the Nazi take-over . . . People were ready for it.' As self-imposed conformity spread, a new social attitude emerged, and at least in some cases transformation took place in a matter of hours, days, or weeks of Hitler's appointment. People out of the country for a brief sojourn were astonished on their return.

Some thought it advisable to make known, without having been asked, that they had no sympathy for the newly proclaimed enemies of the system.

Some thought it advisable to make known, without having been asked, that they had no sympathy for the newly proclaimed enemies of the system. In October 1933, for example, Agnes Meyer, a cashier in a Würzburg grocery, turned in a customer who had insisted on getting the 3 pfennigs owed to her in change. She was accused of having said that she was fed up paying taxes, and especially with laying out money for family allowances. Under questioning by the Gestapo the woman conceded that she might have implied that some people who got such allowances might not have to quibble over small change. Meyer was adamant that an insult to the Führer [Hitler] was intended. Similarly, in late 1943, during an air-raid attack in Kitzingen, Johann Müller, a Catholic with two children, overheard Hugo Engelhardt make the following remark: 'Yes, families with many children should be supported, but with the truncheon. And anyone who had more than three children should be castrated!' Engelhardt was reported and brought to trial. Again, this kind of petty tale-telling went beyond any specific injunction of the regime, and, in both these cases, helped reinforce the system's teachings on population policy.

A Flood of Denunciations

No specific law was ever passed that required citizens to inform on one another, though there was a stipulation in the already existing German criminal code (paragraph 139) that made it a duty to report certain offences one suspected were about to be committed; the law on high treason made a crime out of the failure to communicate to the authorities knowledge of a possible attempt at treason, including threats to Germany's allies, and so on. The presidential decree of 21 March 1933 against malicious attacks on the government, and the law of 20 December 1934 against malicious attacks on the state and Party, were both designed to stop gossiping in public places, but also pertained to private remarks which might be repeated later in public. Neither made denunciation a formal duty, or even mentioned the matter, though both seem to have presupposed that the good citizen would inform upon hearing such gossip. Clauses in the law were so broadly formulated that the most innocuous criticism of the Party, state, its leading personalities or enactments, could conceivably be a basis for denunciation.

Generally speaking, all authorities of party and state reacted positively to those who brought accusations, regardless of how insignificant the allegation, dubious the source, mixed the motives—even if it concerned an act (an anti-Hitler statement, for example) perpetrated prior to 1933, when such behaviour was not even illegal. Although the flood of denunciations at times inclined various institutions to consider insisting upon signed complaints, verbal and even anonymous tips were usually followed up, and, significantly enough, whether the name of the accuser would (if available) be made public was left to the police. In other words, the extent to which an individual had recourse to legal defence, even when the charges were false or carelessly laid, was determined by the Gestapo.

No Unanimous Line Among the Leaders

In discussions with Minister of Justice [Franz] Gürtner in early May 1933, Hitler complained that 'we are living at present in a sea of denunciations and human meanness', when it was not infrequent for one person to condemn another, especially out of economic motives, merely to make capital out of the situation; the resulting worry that one could be turned in for deeds which went back many years was most unfortunate, in that it 'brought monstrous uneasiness in the entire economy'. He added that 'it was not the task of the Third Reich to atone for all the sins' of the Second, so that, especially in the area of economic and tax crime, a line had to be drawn. It was clear to local state officials in Bavaria that, by mid-summer 1933, 'many people feared denunciations and their consequences',—a fear, incidentally, that made it very difficult to gauge public attitudes towards the new National Socialist system. Needless to say, Nazi Party types took advantage of the novel situation to settle accounts with old enemies, and 'ordinary' citizens were not above capitalizing on the opportunity to get rid of business competitors through allegations that led to arrest and internment.

Needless to say, Nazi Party types took advantage of the novel situation to settle accounts with old enemies, and 'ordinary' citizens were not above capitalizing on the opportunity to get rid of business competitors through allegations that led to arrest and internment.

The many false charges from across the country that were evident in the first months of the new regime reached altogether unacceptable proportions by April 1934, when the Reich Minister of the Interior demanded that local authorities take steps to curb the rapid expansion of all denunciations, too many of which were based merely on conflicts with neighbours. He wanted the authorities to prosecute those who made 'thoughtless, invalid complaints' to the police. But at almost the same time (18 April) [Minister] Rudolf Hess announced in a statement that 'every Party and folk comrade impelled by honest concern for the movement and the nation shall have access to the Führer or to me without the risk of being taken to task', a statement openly encouraging even anonymous informers to come forward. During the peacetime years the flood of reports continued without apparent respite, against the hopes of anxious contemporary observers. . . .

Even Dubious Hints Were Followed Up

A common assumption about denouncers is that for the most part they are social misfits whose character weaknesses come to light under certain social conditions. . . . It would be a mistake to think that in Nazi Germany denouncers were only or even primarily drawn from the margins of society.

It also needs to be said that, just as almost all aspects of social life in the Third Reich were politicized, so too were the tales told by the chronic complainers, the grumblers, and the petty gossipers. The Würzburg authorities no longer dismissed their charges as trivial or obvious nonsense. These people, with a degree of social power they never had before, now saw how they might win arguments, settle scores, pay off debts, get rid of bothersome people, all with the help of the Gestapo. It was expeditious to come up with a politically relevant charge, but even the suggestion to the police that something 'suspicious' was in the air would work for a time. Even when the police were confronted with unsavoury characters they generally proceeded as though there might be something in the allegations. From Würzburg in early 1935 comes a case where a family reported their neighbour, Hans Fichtel, for allegedly having said 'to hell with' the Swastika flag! The charge was taken up by the Gestapo even though the family who made it were known to the police—to the whole city, for that matter—for their false accusations. 'The entire family, because of its many previous convictions, had been ostracized in Würzburg and must now be supported by the welfare office.' This reputation did not prevent their charges against Fichtel from being followed up.

[Historian] Reinhard Mann's quantitative analysis of Gestapo cases shows up the alarming consequences that such denunciations could have for the victim. He found that of all those people reported to the police out of personal motives, one quarter were provisionally arrested and spent an average of three days in custody until the baselessness of the charges could be established. Even in those instances where nothing quite so drastic took place, Mann correctly points out that merely being cross-examined by the Gestapo, especially if it took place at headquarters, was already a dreadful experience. One need only reflect on the sinister reputation of the police, the uncertainty of the outcome, the incalculability of the procedure, and the admissibility of evidence about statements made before 1933. . . .

Students Reported Teachers and Parents

Students were among the first to bring information to the Würzburg Gestapo. In April 1933 a group of high-school students charged that their teacher, Dr Georg Kepner, who was then living in Nuremberg, had forbidden them to wear their Nazi emblems in school. Kepner admitted having said—*before* Hitler's appointment—that wearing the emblems might be taken as insulting to the Jewish students in class. In fact, the propensity of schoolchildren to denounce teachers who had disciplined them threatened to get out of hand on some occasions, if the complaints in Bavaria can be taken as representative. A circular from the Ministry of Education of 16 June 1936 noted with alarm that 'students, without the knowledge of their parents, are reporting to the police, or at another convenient place known to them, that their teachers have displayed political unreliability or even a treasonous attitude. The reporters are often students who have had to be disciplined during instruction.' Though many of the charges turned out to be without foundation, they were damaging to the schools' reputation. The ministry wanted such complaints to be handled internally, in the first instance at least, by the local school administration. Needless to say, enforcing such a policy was difficult, if not impossible—not least because of the many ways a determined student could find to lodge a complaint. Not only unruly students reported on their teachers; some diligent pupils also informed. According to many accounts, members of the various branches of the Hitler Youth, down to the lowest levels, were particularly keen to denounce teachers, religious instructors, and, on occasions, even their parents.

In due course some of the heterogeneous group described above as the 'social misfits' were themselves termed 'enemies of the community'. Had the regime lasted longer, this loosely defined category of people would surely have been subjected to treatment much like the kind administered to the Jews and others.

'Race Crimes'

One final point concerning the relationship of these characters and the regime's police system needs to be mentioned. Local police officials could always exercise their prerogative to follow up denunciations. However, the Gestapo acted far more rigorously in cases of accusations against 'opponents'. The police's level of tolerance was at its lowest when it came to any hint of 'race crimes'. Jews and other racial 'outgroups', such as the Poles, Eastern workers, and prisoners of war, were held in particular contempt. Before too long the Gestapo was paying attention to the town drunk, the workshy person, the man always at loggerheads with his neighbours, who wanted to complain about a Pole who was riding a bicycle or drinking at the local pub. But one should avoid concluding that denunciations were chiefly the work of the misfits one might expect to find in any society. For one thing, in Nazi Germany there were an awful lot of 'social misfits': it is safe to say that in this period their numbers swelled to include people who would normally not be so labelled. However, solid citizens, such as teachers, priests, and medical doctors, also denounced 'crimes' that came to their attention. During a visit to their family doctor in Schweinfurt in August 1941, the father of a 15-year-old young girl told the doctor that a Polish foreign worker had made her pregnant. 'In order to protect the remaining youth in the area' the doctor reported the matter to the magistrate, who passed it on to the Gestapo. After 'hard-nosed lying', the deed was admitted under questioning, and not one but two Polish workers were sent to a concentration camp, where they died from 'special handling'. The . . . cases cited by Minister of Justice [Otto Georg] Thierack as examples of the dubious use of denunciation include no marginal social types. There were (1) a 46-year-old technical school teacher and his wife; (2) a husband and wife in their thirties, both medical doctors; (3) a merchant *(Kaufmann)* and his wife; (4) a lawyer and his wife; and (5) a Nazi Party official, listed simply as a 'camp-leader' *(Lagerführer)*, and spouse. If anything linked these people, it was not an inferior social status.

The Nazi regime criminalized any behaviour that might have an oppositional aspect to it. Apart from helping the regime to enforce policies of all kinds, this practice, as [historian] Peter Hüttenberger explains, permitted the regime to pick up 'dissatisfaction of the population in areas where social assistance was not effective': thereby, the regime 'strengthened its domination down to the lowest levels of society, in that it picked up non-conforming types of behaviour that were already developing and, by isolating the individual concerned, destroyed them. The denunciation constituted an important precondition for this.'

One might have expected more attention to popular forms of denunciation in the many books recently devoted to the 'history of everyday life' and those that focus upon 'resistance and persecution'. However, for the most part, such studies tend to touch on the police only in passing. . . .

The motives for offering information to the authorities ranged across the spectrum from base, selfish, personal, to lofty and 'idealistic'. The records project an image of the denouncers—who, not surprisingly, tended to come from the same milieu as those on whom they informed—as drawn largely from groups at the lower end of the social scale. This image is probably correct, but must be qualified lest these groups be judged too harshly. It needs to be borne in mind that upper-income groups and the nobility for the most part did not need to utilize the police, since they had other and more effective avenues through which to exercise social power. Moreover, the police, themselves largely drawn from the lower social orders, were more deferential in cases involving the nobility and the upper bourgeoisie, and pursued individuals from the lower end of the social hierarchy with greater alacrity. Even so, individuals from all social classes offered information to the police. The regime was bound to have second thoughts about this participation when, at times, it was inundated with charges, too many of which were careless or just plain false. But, despite some misgivings, it was felt better to have too much information and co-operation than too little.

5

Why I Dislike Democracy

Adolf Hitler

The following piece is an excerpt from Adolf Hitler's book *Mein Kampf*, the title of which translates as "my struggle." In this book, which he wrote while imprisoned for his part in a 1923 attempt at overthrowing the government, Hitler explains how he came to have little respect for the democratic method of parliamentarianism. As he tells the story, when he already had misgivings about the representation of Germans in the Austrian parliament, he attended sessions of the House of Deputies and laughed at the proceedings. He goes on to raise questions about individual responsibility and representation, arguing that when decisions are made by an elected body, as in a democracy, no one can be held truly responsible for them. Furthermore, according to Hitler, the democratic system threatens to substitute group mediocrity for individual genius.

W hen, not yet twenty years old, I set foot for the first time in the magnificent [Austrian parliament] building on the Franzensring to attend a session of the House of Deputies as a spectator and listener, I was seized with the most conflicting sentiments.

I had always hated parliament, but not as an institution in itself. On the contrary, as a freedom-loving man I could not even conceive of any other possibility of government, for the idea of any sort of dictatorship would . . . have seemed to me a crime against freedom and all reason.

What contributed no little to this was that as a young man, in consequence of my extensive newspaper reading, I had, without myself realizing it, been inoculated with a certain admiration for the British Parliament, of which I was not easily able to rid myself. The dignity with which the Lower House there fulfilled its tasks (as was so touchingly described in our press) impressed me immensely. Could a people have any more exalted form of self-government?

Critical of Austrian Parliamentarianism

But for this very reason I was an enemy of the Austrian parliament. I considered its whole mode of conduct unworthy of the great example. To this the following was now added:

The fate of the Germans in the Austrian state was dependent on their position in the Reichsrat [upper house of the Austrian parliament]. Up to the introduction of universal and secret suffrage, the Germans had had a majority, though an insignificant one, in parliament. Even this condition was precarious, for the Social Democrats, with their unreliable attitude in national questions, always turned against German interests in critical matters affecting the Germans—in order not to alienate the members of the various foreign nationalities. Even in those days the Social Democracy could not be regarded as a German party. And with the introduction of universal suffrage the German superiority ceased even in a purely numerical sense. There was no longer any obstacle in the path of the further de-Germanization of the state.

A few deputies were in their places, yawning at one another; one was 'speaking.'

For this reason my instinct of national self-preservation caused me even in those days to have little love for a representative body in which the Germans were always misrepresented rather than represented. Yet these were deficiencies which, like so many others, were attributable, not to the thing in itself, but to the Austrian state. I still believed that if a German majority were restored in the representative bodies, there would no longer be any reason for a principled opposition to them, that is, as long as the old state continued to exist at all.

These were my inner sentiments when for the first time I set foot in these halls as hallowed as they were disputed. For me, to be sure, they were hallowed only by the lofty beauty of the magnificent building. A Hellenic miracle on German soil!

How soon was I to grow indignant when I saw the lamentable comedy that unfolded beneath my eyes!

Watching Democratic Politicians

Present were a few hundred of these popular representatives who had to take a position on a question of most vital economic importance.

The very first day was enough to stimulate me to thought for weeks on end.

The intellectual content of what these men said was on a really depressing level, in so far as you could understand their babbling at all; for several of the gentlemen did not speak German, but their native Slavic languages or rather dialects. I now had occasion to hear with my own ears what previously I had known only from reading the newspapers. A wild gesticulating mass screaming all at once in every different key, presided over by a good-natured old uncle who was striving in the sweat of his brow to revive the dignity of the House by violently ringing his bell and alternating gentle reproofs with grave admonitions.

I couldn't help laughing.

A few weeks later I was in the House again. The picture was changed beyond recognition. The hall was absolutely empty. Down below everybody was asleep. A few deputies were in their places, yawning at one another; one was 'speaking.' A vice-president of the House was present, looking into the hall with obvious boredom.

The first misgivings arose in me. From now on, whenever time offered me the slightest opportunity, I went back and, with silence and attention, viewed whatever picture presented itself, listened to the speeches in so far as they were intelligible, studied the more or less intelligent faces of the elect of the peoples of this woe-begone state—and little by little formed my own ideas.

Against All Parliamentarianism

A year of this tranquil observation sufficed totally to change or eliminate my former view of the nature of this institution. My innermost position was no longer against the misshapen form which this idea assumed in Austria; no, by now I could no longer accept the parliament as such. Up till then I had seen the misfortune of the Austrian parliament in the absence of a German majority; now I saw that its ruination lay in the whole nature and essence of the institution as such.

A whole series of questions rose up in me.

I began to make myself familiar with the democratic principle of majority rule as the foundation of this whole institution, but devoted no less attention to the intellectual and moral values of these gentlemen, supposedly the elect of the nations, who were expected to serve this purpose.

Thus I came to know the institution and its representatives at once.

In the course of a few years, my knowledge and insight shaped a plastic model of that most dignified phenomenon of modern times: the parliamentarian. He began to impress himself upon me in a form which has never since been subjected to any essential change.

Here again the visual instruction of practical reality had prevented me from being stifled by a theory which at first sight seemed seductive to so many, but which none the less must be counted among the symptoms of human degeneration.

The Western democracy of today is the forerunner of Marxism which without it would not be thinkable. It provides this world plague with the culture in which its germs can spread. In its most extreme form, parliamentarianism created a 'monstrosity of excrement and fire,' in which, however, sad to say, the 'fire' seems to me at the moment to be burned out.

Isn't the very idea of responsibility bound up with the individual?

I must be more than thankful to Fate for laying this question before me while I was in Vienna, for I fear that in Germany at that time I would have found the answer too easily. For if I had first encountered this absurd institution known as 'parliament' in Berlin, I might have fallen into the opposite fallacy, and not without seemingly good cause have sided with those who saw the salvation of the people and the Reich exclusively in furthering the power of the imperial idea, and who nevertheless were alien and blind at once to the times and the people involved.

In Austria this was impossible.

Here it was not so easy to go from one mistake to the other. If parliament was worthless, the Habsburgs [Austrian monarchs] were even more worthless—in no event, less so. To reject 'parliamentarianism' was not enough, for the question still remained open: what then? The rejection and abolition of the Reichsrat would have left the House of Habsburg the sole governing force, a thought which, especially for me, was utterly intolerable.

Questions Come Up

The difficulty of this special case led me to a more thorough contemplation of the problem as such than would otherwise have been likely at such tender years.

What gave me most food for thought was the obvious absence of any responsibility in a single person.

The parliament arrives at some decision whose consequences may be ever so ruinous—nobody bears any responsibility for this, no one can be taken to account. For can it be called an acceptance of responsibility if, after an unparalleled catastrophe, the guilty government resigns? Or if the coalition changes, or even if parliament is itself dissolved?

Can a fluctuating majority of people ever be made responsible in any case?

Isn't the very idea of responsibility bound up with the individual?

But can an individual directing a government be made practically responsible for actions whose preparation and execution must be set exclusively to the account of the will and inclination of a multitude of men?

Or will not the task of a leading statesman be seen, not in the birth of a creative idea or plan as such, but rather in the art of making the brilliance of his projects intelligible to a herd of sheep and blockheads, and subsequently begging for their kind approval?

Is it the criterion of the statesman that he should possess the art of persuasion in as high degree as that of political intelligence in formulating great policies or decisions? Is the incapacity of a leader shown by the fact that he does not succeed in winning for a certain idea the majority of a mob thrown together by more or less savory accidents?

Indeed, has this mob ever understood an idea before success proclaimed its greatness?

Wondering About Representatives

Isn't every deed of genius in this world a visible protest of genius against the inertia of the mass?

And what should the statesman do, who does not succeed in gaining the favor of this mob for his plans by flattery?

Should he buy it?

Or, in view of the stupidity of his fellow citizens, should he renounce the execution of the tasks which he has recognized to be vital necessities? Should he resign or should he remain at his post?

In such a case, doesn't a man of true character find himself in a hopeless conflict between knowledge and decency, or rather honest conviction?

Where is the dividing line between his duty toward the general public and his duty toward his personal honor?

Mustn't every true leader refuse to be thus degraded to the level of a political gangster?

And, conversely, mustn't every gangster feel that he is cut out for politics, since it is never he, but some intangible mob, which has to bear the ultimate responsibility?

Mustn't our principle of parliamentary majorities lead to the demolition of any idea of leadership?

Does anyone believe that the progress of this world springs from the mind of majorities and not from the brains of individuals?

Or does anyone expect that the future will be able to dispense with this premise of human culture?

Does it not, on the contrary, today seem more indispensable than ever?

By rejecting the authority of the individual and replacing it by the numbers of some momentary mob, the parliamentary principle of majority rule sins against the basic aristocratic principle of Nature, though it must be said that this view is not necessarily embodied in the present-day decadence of our upper ten thousand.

Chapter 2

Hitler's Seizure of Power

1

Hitler Used Oratory and Spectacle to Win Followers

Jackson J. Spielvogel

In this selection, Jackson J. Spielvogel, professor emeritus at Pennsylvania State University and author of several books on German history, discusses the messianic aspect of Hitler. According to Spielvogel, Hitler crafted an image of himself as the savior of the German people, and the population, to a considerable extent, accepted him as their messiah. Spielvogel argues that Hitler's success hinged upon his powerful oratory skills which, by appealing to the emotion rather than the intellect, roused deep passions in his listeners and convinced them of his greatness. Also, Spielvogel says, elaborate use of propaganda that promoted clear and simple ideas had a tremendous impact. As an example of such propaganda, Spielvogel specifically focuses on the carefully planned Nuremberg Party Rallies, which were designed to display unity and determination in order to strengthen and enlarge Nazi support in the population.

A dolf Hitler came to regard himself as a man singled out by Providence for a special mission, and he clothed himself in the mantle of a messiah. He claimed that his awareness of his special position dated from 1919, when he lay temporarily blinded in a military hospital. He contended that he had received a "divine mandate" to "liberate the German people and make Germany great." Subsequent speeches reinforced this sense of mission. At his trial in 1924

Jackson J. Spielvogel, *Hitler and Nazi Germany: A History*. Upper Saddle River, NJ: Prentice-Hall, 1992. Copyright © 1992 by Prentice-Hall, Inc. Reproduced by permission of Pearson Education, Inc., Upper Saddle River, New Jersey.

after the abortive Beer Hall Putsch, Hitler said: "The man who is born to be a dictator is not compelled, he wills it. He is not driven forward, but drives himself." In the early days of his movement Hitler likened himself to Jesus: "Just like Christ, I have a duty to my own people." After his accession to the chancellorship in 1933, Hitler's sense of mission grew with every increase in his power. At Würzburg in 1937, he exclaimed to his audience:

> I see clearly what man can do and where his limitations lie, but I am convinced that men who are created by God should live in accordance with the will of the Almighty. However weak the individual may be in the last resort in his whole being and action when compared with the omnipotence and will of Providence, yet at the moment when he acts as this Providence would have him act he becomes immeasurably strong. Then there streams down upon him that force which has marked all greatness in the world's history. And when I look back only on the five years which lie behind us then I feel that I am justified in saying: That has not been the achievement of men alone! If Providence had not guided us I could often never have found these dizzy paths. And that should be recognized especially by our critics! Thus it is that we National Socialists, too, have in the depths of our hearts our faith. We cannot do otherwise: no man can fashion world-history or the history of peoples unless upon his purpose and his powers there rests the blessing of this Providence.

The failure of the attempts on his life reinforced Hitler's conviction of his "divine mission." After the abortive attempt of July 20, 1944, to kill him with a bomb, Hitler remarked to an aide: "Now the almighty has stayed their [the assassins'] hands once more. Don't you agree I should consider it as a nod of Fate that it intends to preserve me for my assigned task?" And to his valet: "That is new proof that I have been selected from among other men by Providence to lead greater Germany to victory."

Further, Hitler saw National Socialism not so much as a political movement; "rather we are a religion." The use of sacred oaths of allegiance, the Blood Flag ceremony as a religious ritual, the Nazi holy days as substitutes for traditional religious holidays, and the call for miracles of faith were all manifestations of Nazism's quasi-religious character.

Many Germans shared Hitler's vision of himself as their messiah. The American journalist William Shirer, an observer of Hitler's triumphant entry into Nuremberg for a party rally, grasped this aspect of Nazism in Germany:

> About ten o'clock tonight I got caught in a mob of ten thousand hysterics who jammed the moat in front of Hitler's hotel, shouting: "We want our Führer." I was a little shocked at the faces, especially those of the women when Hitler finally appeared on the balcony for a moment. They reminded me of the crazed expressions I saw once in the back country of Louisiana on the faces of some Holy Rollers who were about to hit the trail. They looked up at him as if he were a Messiah, their faces transformed into something positively inhuman. If he had remained in sight for more than a few moments, I think many of the women would have swooned from excitement.

Nazi leaders encouraged this messianic view of Hitler in the German schools. Children were required after 1934 to write out compositions comparing Hitler to Jesus. The Hitler *Jungvolk*, one of the youth organizations for boys, used the following song:

> Adolf Hitler is our Saviour, our hero
> He is the noblest being in the whole wide world.
> For Hitler we live,
> For Hitler we die.
> Our Hitler is our Lord
> Who rules a brave new world.

Such adoration inspired a cult of Hitler as the new messiah of a reborn Germany.

Hitler's Powerful Speeches

Hitler's ability as an orator was a major reason for his success. His oratorical triumphs emerged out of two contrasting elements—his natural capacity to arouse deep and passionate emotions in his listeners and his careful preparation of his speeches and their setting. Hitler did possess a mysterious aptitude to read the mind of his audience. The importance of this sensitivity to assembled crowds was stressed in

Mein Kampf: "He [the orator] will always let himself be borne along by the great masses in such a way that instinctively the very words come to his lips that he needs to speak to the hearts of his audience." Hitler believed that he was the greatest practitioner of his own words. As he told Hermann Rauschning [a Nazi politician who later defected], "I am conscious that I have no equal in the art of swaying the masses." Although his speeches were carefully structured and he used notes in delivering them, he was not restricted by these preparations. It took him ten to fifteen minutes "to inhale the feelings of his audience," as he stated it. Having done this, he expressed to his listeners their deepest dreams and desires. Otto Strasser, an early member of the northern wing of the Nazi party and later a critic of Hitler, described the process well:

> Hitler responds to the vibration of the human heart with the delicacy of a seismograph, or perhaps of a wireless receiving set, enabling him, with a certainty with which no conscious gift could endow him, to act as a loudspeaker proclaiming the most secret desires, the least admissible instincts, the sufferings and personal revolts of a whole nation. . . . I have been asked many times what is the secret of Hitler's extraordinary power as a speaker. I can only attribute it to his uncanny intuition, which infallibly diagnoses the ills from which his audience is suffering. If he tries to bolster up his argument with theories or quotations from books he has only imperfectly understood, he scarcely rises above a very poor mediocrity. But let him throw away his crutches and step out boldly, speaking as the spirit moves him, and he is promptly transformed into one of the greatest speakers of the century. . . . Adolf Hitler enters a hall. He sniffs the air. For a minute he gropes, feels his way, senses the atmosphere. Suddenly he bursts forth. . . . His words go like an arrow to their target, he touches each private wound in the raw, liberating the mass unconscious, expressing its innermost aspirations, telling it what it most wants to hear.

It was not unusual for people to describe their reactions to Hitler's speeches in sexual and religious overtones. One writer spoke of Hitler's speeches as "sex murders"; and others used the vocabulary of sexual experience, including such words as *climax, discharge,* and *mass orgasm,* to describe the interaction of Hitler and the crowds during his speeches. Some used religious terminology. Consider this description by businessman Kurt Ludecke:

> Presently my critical faculty was swept away. . . . I do not know how to describe the emotions that swept over me as I heard this man. His words were like a scourge. When he spoke of the disgrace of Germany, I felt ready to spring on any enemy. His appeal to German manhood was like a call to arms, the gospel he preached a sacred truth. He seemed another Luther. I forgot everything but the man; then, glancing around, I saw that his magnetism was holding these thousands as one. Of course, I was ripe for this experience. I was a man of thirty-one, weary of disgust and disillusionment, a wanderer seeking a cause; a patriot without a channel for his patriotism, a yearner after the heroic without a hero. The intense will of the man, the passion of his sincerity seemed to flow from him into me. I experienced an exaltation that could be likened only to religious conversion. I felt sure that no one who had heard Hitler that afternoon could doubt that he was a man of destiny, the vitalizing force in the future of Germany.

Generating such an emotional response from his audience required an intensity of effort that left Hitler drenched in sweat and totally drained at the end of a speech. He sometimes lost five pounds in the process. His associates always described him as unable to function in any normal fashion after speaking.

Attention to Details

Hitler has often been compared to a medium or a shaman in his uncanny abilities with an audience, but there was also deliberation behind most aspects of his public speeches. The man who created emotional reactions by gesticulating wildly as if out of control was the same man who worked constantly to be in control—a feat he accomplished, first of all, by improving his techniques of public speaking. Supposedly, Hitler studied the example of a Munich entertainer for gaining the attention of rowdy beer-cellar crowds. One of Hitler's early biographers recounts that Hitler often practiced gesturing in front of a mirror in his Munich room on the Thierschstrasse. He spent hours in a studio being photographed by the party photographer, Heinrich Hoffmann, in a variety of posed gestures. After examining the photos, he utilized in his speaking engagements those gestures that looked attractive to him.

Generating such an emotional response from his audience required an intensity of effort that left Hitler drenched in sweat and totally drained at the end of a speech. He sometimes lost five pounds in the process.

To augment his effectiveness as a speaker, Hitler paid equal attention to the physical environment in which his speeches were given. Early in his career, he checked the acoustics of the major beer halls in Munich so that he could adjust the loudness of his voice to each one. He also examined the ventilation and physical arrangement of the rooms. As the party grew and Hitler's oratory became more important he continued to busy himself with the trappings of his

With his powerful oratory skills, Hitler was able to arouse deep passions in his listeners. Here, he addresses a group of Hitler Youth.

gatherings. The theatrical element became paramount. Official party guidelines were established for every meeting: halls should always be too small rather than too large to create the effect of being overwhelmed by supporters; at least one-third of the audience should be party followers; nighttime was better than daytime because the emotional effect on the listeners would be greater in the evening; people were to be kept waiting for Hitler in order to increase the air of expectation and the joy when he arrived; and Hitler would enter triumphantly without introductory speeches so that all interest would be focused on the leader. All these effects were calculated to heighten Hitler's emotional impact on the audience.

The content of Hitler's speeches remained remarkably consistent. Before coming to power, Hitler did present his favorite ideological concerns, especially anti-Semitism and *Lebensraum* [living space], but he also emphasized general subjects as well. He condemned the present and pointed to all the signs of Germany's disintegration and ruin—the danger of Marxism, the weaknesses of the government, the humiliation of Germany in the dictated peace of Versailles, corruption in everyday affairs, the large number of unemployed, wretched, and hungry ("Germany is starving on democracy"), and the decadence of the West, from which the Weimar Republic stemmed. In a speech of 1932:

> Starting with the day of the Revolution up to the epoch of subjugation and enslavement, up to the time of treaties and emergency decrees, we see failure upon failure, collapse upon collapse, misery upon misery. Timidity, lethargy and hopelessness are everywhere the milestones of these disasters. . . . The peasantry today is ground down, industry is collapsing, millions have lost their saved pennies, millions of others are unemployed. Everything that formerly stood firm has changed, everything that formerly seemed great has been overthrown. Only one thing has remained preserved for us: the men and the parties who are responsible for the misfortunes. They are still here to this day.

Hitler's speeches contained negative themes: "There is only defiance and hate, hate and again hate." "No, we forgive nothing; we demand revenge." But there was as well a very positive element in Hitler's speeches: his visionary images for the future. Germany could be great again if it were unified with a strong government led by a party that would have a free hand in domestic and foreign policy. Nazism was portrayed as the movement that could unify the nation, create racial and national rebirth, and lead Germany back to greatness. *Fatherland, honor, greatness,* and *power* were key words in Hitler's appeal. . . .

The Role of Propaganda

Adolf Hitler was a man obsessed by a set of ideas that he wished to translate into reality. This ideal necessitated molding the German people into a unit that would follow him under any circumstances. Propaganda and mass rallies were the instruments by which the Germans could be prepared for the tremendous tasks that lay before them.

It was reported that at the 1937 rally a group of foreign correspondents were so overcome by emotion that they rose to their feet with arms raised in the Nazi salute and joined in the singing of "Deutschland, Deutschland über Alles" [the national anthem].

Hitler had taken an acute interest in the use of propaganda when he first began to study political events, presumably in Vienna. World War I, however, convinced him of the enormous significance of a well-developed propaganda campaign. In *Mein Kampf,* Hitler elaborated his basic principles for effective propaganda. Propaganda must be addressed not to the intellectuals of society but only to the masses. "The function of propaganda does not lie in the scientific training of the individual, but in calling the masses' attention to certain facts." Since its appeal was directed to the masses, it must be "aimed at the emotions and only to a very limited degree to the so-called intellect." Its intellectual level needs to be adjusted to "the most limited intelligence among those it is addressed to." For Hitler, this "limited intelligence" of the masses meant that effective propaganda had to rely on constant repetition of a few basic points, since "only after the simplest ideas are repeated thousands of times will the masses finally remember them."

Hitler perceived the psychological importance of mass meetings in creating support for a movement. They offered a sense of community that satisfied the need to belong to a larger group, and subsequently gave greater meaning to life. In the mass meeting "the individual, who at first, while becoming a supporter of a young movement, feels lonely and easily succumbs to the fear of being alone, for the first time gets the picture of a larger community, which in most people has a strengthening, encouraging effect." Hitler realized that mass meetings had such emotional effects that people came away from them with stronger convictions than ever before:

> When from his little workshop or big factory, in which he [a representative of a new doctrine] feels very small, he steps for the first time into a mass meeting and has thousands and thousands of people of the same opinions around him, when, as a seeker, he is swept away by three or four thousand others into the mighty effect of suggestive intoxication and enthusiasm, when the visible success and agreement of thousands confirm to him the rightness of the new doctrine and for the first time arouse doubt in the truth of his previous conviction— then he himself has succumbed to the magic influence of what we designate as "mass suggestion." The will, the longing, and also the power of thousands are accumulated in every individual. The man who enters such a meeting doubting and wavering leaves it inwardly reinforced: he has become a link in the community.

Hitler's convictions about propaganda and mass spectacles quickly became public policy in the Third Reich. His willingness to establish a Ministry for Public Enlightenment and Propaganda under Joseph Goebbels demonstrated his admiration for propaganda. It was, after all, the means to manipulate the German people to any end, as Hitler revealed in a secret speech to the editors of the domestic press in 1938:

> Circumstances have forced me to talk almost exclusively of peace for decades. . . . It has now become necessary to psychologically change the German people's course in a gradual way and slowly make it realize that there are things that must . . . be carried through by

the methods of force and violence. . . . This work has required months, it was begun systematically; it is being continued and reinforced. . . .

The Nuremberg Party Rallies

Of all the mass gatherings staged in Nazi Germany, the Nuremberg rallies, known as the *Parteitage*, or party days, became the most spectacular. The first party day had been held in Munich in 1923. Its purpose was to bring together party members in order to show the strength of the organization and to attract popular support, including that of other right-wing political groups. Beginning in 1927, the *Parteitag* was held every September in Nuremberg; the last one took place there in 1938. From 1934 on, the rallies lasted for a week. Nuremberg was chosen because of its historical symbolism. It had been one of the leading German cities of the Holy Roman Empire in the late Middle Ages and the Reformation period and became the embodiment of national ideals in the nineteenth century. By holding modern rallies in historic "Old German" settings, Hitler hoped to fuse past and present into a new cultural unity.

Practices introduced during the party days of the 1920s were used in the gigantic rallies of the 1930s. In the *Fahnenweihe* (consecration of the flags) ceremony, the original flag of the party, which had been carried by the SA during the Beer Hall Putsch and was stained with the blood of Nazis wounded in the street fighting, was touched to new flags, initiating them for use as party banners. Richard Wagner's music and Wagnerian stage effects were also introduced in the 1920s. What was significantly different about the rallies of that decade from the later ones was Hitler's blatant proclamation of the real aims of the Nazi program—anti-Semitism, the annexation of German-speaking territories in Europe, stringent nationalism, and ruthless destruction of the enemies of National Socialism. The latter included Marxism, the Jews, pacifism, the Weimar Republic, the parliamentary system, and international capitalism. In the 1923 rally, Hitler said: "After our reckoning [with foreign and domestic enemies] we will divide the people into Germans and non-Germans. The German traits will be successful, and we will destroy what is non-German." In these early rallies, Hitler appeared as the revolutionary visionary. . . .

The Nuremberg rallies had an enormous impact on all

who participated in them, including Hitler. The adulation and deification of Hitler at Nuremberg fed his own messianic image of himself and increased his megalomaniacal tendencies. At the 1936 party day, he expressed his feeling of deep mystical communion with the crowds at Nuremberg:

> Do we not feel once again in this hour the miracle that brought us together? Once you heard the voice of a man, and it struck deep into your hearts; it awakened you, and you followed this voice. Year after year you went after it, though him who had spoken you never even saw. You heard only a voice, and you followed it. When we meet each other here, the wonder of our coming together fills us all. Not everyone of you sees me, and I do not see everyone of you. But I feel you, and you feel me. It is the belief in our people that has made us small men great, that has made us poor men rich, that has made brave and courageous men out of us wavering, spiritless, timid folk; this belief made us see our road when we were astray; it joined us together into one whole! . . . You come, that . . . you may, once in a while, gain the feeling that now we are together; we are with him and he with us, and we are now Germany!

The Germans present at Nuremberg reciprocated his sentiments, reflected for all of them in the chants of the Labor Service Corps: "We want one leader! Nothing for us! Everything for Germany! *Heil* Hitler!" Even foreigners seem to have been affected by the passions engendered by these rallies. Thus these observations by French ambassador François-Poncet:

> Seven years yearly Nuremberg was a city devoted to revelry and madness; almost a city of convulsionaries, Holy Rollers and the like. The surroundings, the beauty of the spectacles presented, and the luxury of the hospitality offered exerted a strong influence upon the foreigners whom the Nazi Government was careful to invite annually. Many visitors, dazzled by Nazi display, were infected by the virus of Nazism. They returned home convinced by the doctrine and filled with admiration for the performance.

It was reported that at the 1937 rally a group of foreign correspondents were so overcome by emotion that they rose to their feet with arms raised in the Nazi salute and joined in the singing of "Deutschland, Deutschland über Alles" [the national anthem].

In his book on the Nuremberg rallies, [historian] Hamilton Burden concluded that they

> will probably remain one of the most startling chapters of twentieth-century history. They are a frightening example of the awesome power of modern propaganda techniques. Borrowing from pagan cults, church rituals, and Wagnerian theater, and other ways of reaching the thoughts and dreams of the masses, the absolute state perfected, in Nuremberg, its ability to dominate man's mind.

What Burden says about the Nuremberg party days can be said equally about the other mass rallies set up by Hitler and the Nazis. If the mass meetings before 1933 were aimed at creating the kind of emotional upheaval that would lead millions to vote Hitler into power, then the mass spectacles after Hitler came to power were directed at creating an atmosphere in which Germans would become fanatically dedicated to Hitler and to their unity in a truly Germanic *Volksgemeinschaft* [the Nazi term for an ideal German society]. Hitler repeatedly expressed the need for unity, harmony, discipline, will power, and obedience, and many Germans clearly became enthusiastically committed to those ideas in response.

To Hitler, the successful realization of his ideology called for an active foreign policy based ultimately on expansion achieved by war. The German people had to be made willing and able tools for executing that foreign policy. To Hitler that could be achieved only if the German race could be purified of the Jews and made into such a unified whole that Germans would consciously renounce their individuality and submerge their wills with that of Germany and the Führer [leader]. The mass spectacles, with their "awesome power of modern propaganda techniques," became a major instrument in achieving Hitler's goal of educating the German people to his new state and its ideals. That Hitler conquered as much of Europe as he did and convinced the German people to assist him in annihilating the Jews and to hold out against the Allies as long as they did certainly proves that he came frighteningly close to accomplishing that goal.

2

Hitler's Opponents Unwittingly Aided His Rise to Power

Robert G.L. Waite

In this piece, historian Robert G.L. Waite argues that Hitler's rise to power was far from inevitable. According to Waite, the other political parties and politicans, rather than Hitler and the Nazis, were most responsible for his coming to power. Waite argues that neither the other important Weimar parties, such as the Social Democrats or the Christian Center Party, nor individual powerful politicians, such as Chancellor Heinrich Brüning or President Paul von Hindenburg, did anything to prevent Hitler from entering the cabinet and becoming chancellor of Germany. To the contrary, Waite maintains, Hitler's various political opponents were each busy trying to win Hitler over to their side and hoped that he would be easily tamed once he had to carry the responsibility of political power. This piece is taken from Waite's book *The Psychopathic God Adolf Hitler.*

O ne might think that Hitler's attainment of power in 1933 was a foregone conclusion. Apparently all German history had been conspiring to aid him; the economic, social, and psychological crisis following 1930 was obviously pushing him along; the magic of his personality did the rest. And thus was Hitler hailed as savior and swept into power by a mesmerized and ecstatic people. But it did not happen that way. The strange career of Adolf Hitler provides many

Robert G.L. Waite, *The Psychopathic God: Adolf Hitler.* New York: Basic Books, 1977. Copyright © 1977 by Robert G.L. Waite. Reproduced by permission of Basic Books, a member of Perseus Books, LLC.

insights into the vagaries of history, and this is one of them: not even he was inevitable.

The combination of past history, present crisis, and charismatic personality helps explain why Hitler had become such a political force by the fall of 1932. But none of this explains *how* he actually became Führer [German term for leader, often used to refer to Hitler] of Germany. He was not voted into power by the German people, nor did he seize power, as Nazi legend later asserted, by a heroic *Machtergreifung* [seizure of power]. Political power was handed to him in a sordid political deal.

He had tried three different ways to attain his goal. First, he had sought to seize power by coup d'état in 1923; he had failed in that memorable fiasco. Second, he had tried to win a mandate from the German people; but he had failed to win the simple majority he had promised President von Hindenburg. The best he could do in the summer of 1932 was to get 37.4 percent of the vote. And even after attaining the chancellorship, profiting from the Reichstag [name of the parliament building] fire, and then utilizing all the wiles of [Joseph] Goebbels's propaganda machine, his own brilliant demagoguery, and the intimidating power of his Storm Troopers—even after all that, Hitler could get only 43.9 percent of the vote. A majority of the German people still withheld their confidence from him. True, they had given him more votes than anyone else. But not a majority.

The Responsibility of Weimar Parties

After failing in these efforts, Hitler decided to get into power through intrigue and political deals. [Historian Alan] J.P. Taylor is correct: the answer to the question of *how* Hitler came to power lies less with Hitler and the Nazis than with other parties and politicians. Every one of the political parties of the Republic made a contribution to the death of democracy and the victory of Hitler. There is considerable truth in [cultural critic] Oswald Spengler's scathing comment about the much-trumpeted Nazi triumph: "That was no victory; there was no opposition." The German Communist Party, for example, constituted by 1932 the strongest Communist movement in Europe. Yet it succumbed to Hitler without a struggle. By the summer of 1933 the KPD was dissolved, its leaders jailed, its funds confiscated. Among the reasons for this surprising failure was the strangely erratic policy emanating from Stalin's Kremlin. From 1924 to 1928, the orders were to cooperate with the moderate German Social Democrats; after 1928, orders went out to fight them as "Social Fascists." In this phase, Stalin actually cooperated with Hitler in order to undermine bourgeois democracy. The theory was that once fascism ("the last stage of monopoly capitalism") attained power, the time would be ripe for a final communist takeover. But after helping Hitler into power, the Communist Party took no action at all. [As historian Alan Bullock put it:] "The Party which for fifteen years had talked of nothing but revolution failed when the crisis it had itself prescribed as the revolutionary moment came."

Each group hoped that Hitler would supply the votes and remain the "prisoner" of his "superiors."

The moderate Social Democrats, founders of the Republic and, until 1932, its largest party, were unable or unwilling to act effectively. Seized by apathy bordering on fatalism, they could not or would not act to stop Hitler. "We were driven by the force of circumstance," one leader said pathetically in August 1933. "We were really only the passive object of developments." The moderate socialists later protested that it was not their fault that Hitler came to power—their theoretical Marxist allies, the Communists, had cooperated with Hitler and attacked them instead of helping them. There is truth to the charge, but it overlooks the crucial fact that the Social Democrats themselves had done little to fulfill social promises and had done nothing when, in July 1932, Chancellor [Franz] von Papen and his "Cabinet of the Barons" illegally seized the government of Prussia—two-thirds of Germany. At this time, as later, the moderates lacked the will to take effective action. Totally misjudging the nature of Hitler and his threat, they kept thinking that "the ultimate victory of the working class movement" was indeed inevitable, and that Hitler was merely a passing phenomenon. In accordance with that tradition, they put their faith in the "potential energy of a mass party" and kept reassuring themselves with that

By the fall of 1932, Hitler was a powerful political force in Germany. Here, a large crowd is gathered to hear him speak.

empty and amorphous slogan. A corollary of this belief was that Hitler, as the head of "reactionary forces," would of his own accord disintegrate along with his supporters, whereas the power of the working class was "indestructible."

The conservative parties of the right, which had spent so much of their energies vilifying the Republic, showed that they had no political program of their own except to devise ways to make accommodations with Hitler. By 1932, German conservatism was intellectually sterile and politically bankrupt.

The Role of Chancellor Brüning

The chancellor of the republic during the critical years of 1930–1932 was Dr. Heinrich Brüning of the Catholic Center Party. He has often been portrayed as an able political leader who struggled manfully against the Nazi tide. His record does not support that reputation. He made the critical political mistake of dissolving the Reichstag in 1930 and attempting to rule by emergency presidential decree, thus making his government dependent upon the whim of old President [Paul von] Hindenburg, who was increasingly influenced by a clique of military reactionaries. Brüning's myopic and stubborn policy of deflation exacerbated the Depression, idling factories and throwing millions of workers out on the street. The "Hunger Chancellor" did little to help democracy. The position he had maneuvered himself into between left and right produced this devastating political joke: "Why is Brüning like a guitar? Answer: Because he's held by the left hand and played by the right."

But Brüning may not have been merely inept. Recent studies have raised very serious questions about his purported commitment to democracy and opposition to Hitler. It is now clear that his chief hope as chancellor was to win Hitler's secret support for a restoration of the monarchy; that Cardinal Pacelli, later Pope Pius XII, urged Brüning, a devout Catholic, to make special accommodations with Hitler; and that Brüning himself assisted Hitler in writing one of the Führer's key speeches. The Weimar chancellor's attitude toward Hitler at this time—whatever his later protestations may have been—was well expressed by a statement that shows how totally he misjudged the Führer of the Nazis. On the very eve of the Third Reich, Brüning said: "If Hitler would become chancellor under normal conditions [sic], one could then regard the situation with a certain amount of calm."

That was precisely the problem. The leaders of the democracy in its most desperate hour were not attempting to stop the menace of a Hitler dictatorship or to exclude him from office; rather, all their political energies were expended in efforts to bring him into a cabinet—with each political faction trying to win him over to its side. Each group hoped that Hitler would supply the votes and remain the "prisoner" of his "superiors." All were confident that they knew how to handle him. It was also assumed that once he was involved in the government, the responsibilities of political power would teach him humility and moderation.

It has been said that the story of Hitler's rise to power is the story of his underestimation. It must also be said [as historian Ernst Nolte put it] that "there would have been no story of Hitler at all had not outstanding men and forces estimated him highly—for their own purposes."

Never was vapid expectation more effectively exploited.

3

Hitler Employed a Seductive Strategy of Give and Take

Adam LeBor and Roger Boyes

Children in the Hitler Youth had fun and felt important, yet the Nazi organization was designed to alienate them from their parents. Workers got their own bank holiday and cheap vacations, yet their independent unions disappeared into a large, Nazi-controlled organization. Single and married mothers received official Nazi recognition for their work in industry, but they were told to stay at home and bear more children. The thesis of the following text by journalists Adam LeBor and Roger Boyes is that Hitler managed to seduce the disadvantaged with a clever strategy of give and take.

In 1946 William Emker was a young man stationed with OMGUS (Office of the Military Government of the United States) in Berlin. Out of curiosity he visited Hitler's Reichskanzlei (office), inspecting the bomb damage and shuffling through the scattered papers. The Russians wanted to use the metal filing cabinets and had tipped the documents onto the floor. Emker picked up a letter addressed to 'My dearest Führer' [term meaning *leader* that was used as a synonym for Hitler] and pocketed it. Over the subsequent months Emker travelled about twenty times into the Soviet sector, entered the Reichskanzlei by a side entrance and stuffed bags full of letters to the Führer into his briefcase. For the most part they were love letters, duly

Adam LeBor and Roger Boyes, *Seduced by Hitler*. New York: Sourcebooks, Inc., 2000. Copyright © 2000 by Adam LeBor and Roger Boyes. Reproduced by permission of Sourcebooks, Inc.

registered by the chancellery staff, never shown to Hitler and stored in metal cases. Some of the senders were reported to the Gestapo [the Nazi secret police]. Most were treated with contempt. The letters were addressed to 'My sweet one', 'My dear sugar sweet Adolf', 'My hotly loved dear heart' and were of remarkable intimacy. Friedel S. writing from Hartmannsdorf on 23 April 1939 begged the Führer to father her child. There were thousands of such letters. 'I want to eat you up with my love,' says one woman. 'You are looking for a woman, I need a man,' says another.

Step by step, mothers and fathers were banished from the lives of their children.

Some of these women were plainly demented with loneliness, with the burden of running a household while their husbands were at the front. But the underlying point of these love letters is that they represent the triumph of Hitler's dictatorial style: he wanted to bind all Germans to him personally, to circumvent and ultimately destroy mediating institutions. The traditional family structure, already eroded by the Weimar years, was rendered increasingly outmoded by war and the absence of men. The Nazi party simulated a defence of the German family while actually concocting policies or tolerating behaviour that eroded it. Hitler set out to supplant the personal physical love of a husband with an immaculate love of the Führer. By the same token children were to be given an ersatz Father. Not only the Hitler Youth, but also a whole system of élite schooling loosened ties with parents and brought up many thousands of children according to supposedly manly and Germanic standards, equipping them to be the future leadership of the Reich.

Control over the Children

The seductiveness of this system illustrates the ease with which Hitler attempted to remove one of the key pillars of civil society: parental influence over the upbringing of their children. Some 17,000 children were educated at thirty Napolas (National Political Educational Institutions). In addition there were thirteen Adolf Hitler schools and in Bavaria, a Reichsschule of the NSDAP [Nazi Party]. All mimicked

British public schools and added for good measure a strong flavour of army cadet college. They were almost universally popular with pupils. 'We had a great time,' recalls Count Mainhardt Nayhauss, 'I had ten pairs of shoes and different uniforms, training suits all provided by the state with a minimal contribution from my mother of 75 Reichsmarks, including 5 Rmarks pocket money.' The schools laid great stress on tests of courage. 'In Napola,' remembers Hardy Krüger, 'you had to jump from a 10 meter board into a cold swimming pool. But in the Adolf Hider School I had to swim under the ice of a Berlin lake for 10 meters.' The Adolf Hitler school pupils considered themselves the future élite. 'I assumed that after the Final Victory I would be made, at least, the Gauleiter of Moscow,' jokes Krüger who in fact became an actor. The children were selected on the basis of racial purity, party recommendation and physical fitness. Parents were usually more than happy to have their sons sent to such schools because the quality of normal education had slumped. Male teachers had been called up, funds were diverted and, by the time the bombing raids started, school life was completely dislocated. Hitler took a personal interest in the special schools—the headmaster of an Adolf Hitler school was the only teacher to have regular audiences with him. Plainly Hitler saw the need for an élite fast lane form of education. Although this is an uncontroversial position in Britain and France, in post-war Germany such schools became taboo, firmly identified with the Nazis. The positive memories of school graduates suggest that Hitler knew which emotional buttons should be pressed: how to give boys back their childhood and at the same time subtly prepare them for party service. The party demanded a quid pro quo from the parents. Once a pupil was enrolled he could not be removed from the Adolf Hitler school by his parents. Holiday time disappeared. Letters home were strictly rationed. Step by step, mothers and fathers were banished from the lives of their children and familial loyalty was transferred to the teacher, to the school and to the Führer. . . .

Seduction of the Workers

Hitler's success in winning over the working class was due to a sophisticated reward system, that sufficient numbers of workers were seduced to neutralize resistance. The Nazis understood that the working class was highly segmented, different according to region and industrial sector (there was a huge gap, for example, between the mentality of a Bavarian Catholic truck driver; of a Berlin seamstress; or a Hamburg stevedore). Dividing the workers rather than 'conquering' them became one of the central goals of Nazi social policy as well as the guiding principle of the Gestapo.

The workers in the Third Reich have long been a riddle to historians. The workers, and their parties, Communist and Social Democrat, were the only force in the 1920s and the 1930s that could have blocked the rise and hegemony of the Nazis. Until the last year of the war the regime managed to secure the active or passive support of many sections of the middle class and the various élites. That support fluctuated: the farmers were restless between 1938 and 1940, the educated middle class was upset with the pogroms of November 1938 and there were constant bureaucratic conflicts. But the loyalty of these and other sceptical Germans was won, or bought, and organized resistance was confined to the nooks and crannies of society. The workers may have shifted allegiance from the leftist parties to the Nazis but the defection should be seen as a temporary loan to the new party. The dominant theme of the 1920s was the unbridled power of capital and of speculators, the feeling that ordinary people were vulnerable to the unaccountable manoeuvring of the wealthy (indeed one could argue this remains a dominant concern providing the legitimacy of the post-war East German state and fuelling modern Germany's opposition to globalization). Those who believed the Nazis would shield them from *Wucherkapital*—wild exploitative capitalism— were to be quickly disappointed. The role of capital was strengthened rather than sapped by the Nazis. The question then is why there was no massive protest from within the working class. Why did the working class—the most aggrieved sector of society—not launch at least one major challenge to the regime? . . .

May Day

Hitler's initial plan was . . . to place the unions under the command of a Reichskommissar, preferably someone with social democratic credentials, such as August Winnig, a bullish building worker who had shown some sympathy for the Right. [Reinhold] Muchow [head of the Nazi workers union NSBO] believed he had a better idea for wooing the workers. May Day 1933 should be declared a workers holiday thus fulfilling a long time ambition of the Social Democratic workers' movement. This was a typical seduction technique of Hitler and [Joseph] Goebbels: to hand the workers a triumph and at the same time plot to take away their power. On 16 April Muchow presented to Hitler the timetable for the emasculation of the free, that is Social Democratic, union movement. Hitler approved, though he had no intention of fulfilling Muchow's ambition to be at the head of the new movement. Hitler had earmarked [Robert] Ley, an ex-World War I pilot and a brilliant organizer with a foul temper. . . .

The question then is why there was no massive protest from within the working class.

May Day was a victory for the seducers' art. From early morning the radio broadcast worker songs and worker plays and worker essays. Around 10 million people were on the move—the biggest demonstration ever staged in a non-Communist state. For the first time managers and entrepreneurs could be seen marching arm in arm with blue and white collar workers ('workers of the forehead and the fist' in the Nazi jargon). Not all the workers had been brainwashed. On their way to the Tempelhof, the sprawling aerodrome in the centre of Berlin, two workers stopped off to relieve themselves in a pissoir. As a contemporary reports, they looked at each other and in a few gruff words decided to break away from the overregulated proletarian parade and head home. They were amazed by the numbers of swastikas fluttering from the windows in working class areas.

The End of Independent Unions

The next morning on the dot of ten o'clock the SA brownshirts and the SS stormed into the offices and banks of the social democratic unions and arrested union officials. Files and accounts were carried away in trucks. They were needed to support trumped-up corruption charges against union leaders for abuse of union funds—a crude attempt to turn popular anger against worker leaders. Funds, said Ley, had been used to finance Marxist parties. In one hour the operation was over: the union movement had been decapitated with barely a squeak of protest. Ley and Muchow decided that all unions should join an 'action committee'. Two hundred and thirty-nine union associations had joined up by 5 May.

The DAF, the Deutsche Arbeitsfront, was up and running in the same month. The speed of the action, but also the sharpness of the rhetoric, was almost revolutionary. The point of the DAF was to end class warfare yet it used, initially at least, the muscle-flexing vocabulary of militant socialists. Indeed many employers wondered what had hit them. 'Those industrial magnates still in power should watch their language otherwise they could find themselves swept aside with force,' said a DAF functionary in Muenster. The DAF distributed questionnaires on the shop floor asking for information about wages and working conditions. First wage demands were lodged—for a pay hike in the building industry—and Ley started to talk of the need for a minimum wage. But the intention was clear: to radicalize the workers and offer them a credible alternative not only to social democratic unions but also to the Social Democratic Party itself. By June 1933 the Social Democratic Party was banned and the DAF started to transform itself from a union-like organization with hierarchies built on the shop floor to a mass organization in which everyone was merely a member.

The number of people in work rose by 2.5 million in the same period.

Terror and seduction: the fatal attraction of Hitler. The propaganda machine created a new world, virtual reality, which could be barely recognized by ordinary workers. 'It sounded good yet somehow it seemed to be happening to somebody else,' said one steel worker looking back at 1933 from the perspective of 1947. In most car factories there was full employment, furniture shops were enjoying record sales, cinemas and theatres were flourishing. In 1933 300,000 more marriages were registered than in 1932: an achievement chalked up to Hitler. In November 1933 the number of unemployed dropped to 3.7 million. That was 2.2 million less than at the beginning of the year. The number of people in work rose by 2.5 million in the same period.

That is: the number of unregistered unemployed, the great grey region, was also falling. . . .

Better Working Conditions

Hitler's seductive skills far outweighed the impact of coercion. He recognized that there was no single working class. Many workers were striving towards the middle class. Class solidarity had been destroyed in the Depression. Hitler offered something quite new: the image of an organized work and leisure society in which hard work and loyalty was rewarded in a completely modern manner.

The DAF was the perfect vehicle for this strategy. Under its wings, the Nazis' prime seductive devices *Schönheit der Arbeit* (Beauty of Work) and *Kraft durch Freude* (Strength through Joy) were set up and dangled in front of a disorientated, but ultimately grateful work force. The former promised better working conditions, the latter state-sponsored leisure and recreation. . . .

The Seduction of 'Beauty of Work'

'Bring spring into the factories' was the slogan [of the Beauty of Work campaign, which was undertaken to improve factory environments]. Sports fields and gardens were laid around smoky steel works. Inside day rooms were installed, outside window frames were painted and swimming pools dug. In line with American productivity studies it was ruled that 'good lighting means good work' and Siemens and AEG profited accordingly, decking out shop floors with neon. . . .

National Socialism found a way of combining its motherhood ideology with the illusion of emancipation.

But Beauty of Work was too clumsy a device to seduce workers. The pressure was still on workers to boost productivity and clean lavatories and Beauty of Work did not alter the situation: rather it seemed like an excuse not to pay higher wages. Above all, *Schönheit der Arbeit* had become a bureaucracy. Its inspection teams viewed 70,000 factories, made recommendations, handed out praise and on occasion took bribes for failing to notice cesspits or flaking ceilings. *Schönheit der Arbeit* was treated with the same kind of scepticism that greeted clean up campaigns in Soviet Russia in the 1970s. Work, quite simply, was not supposed to be beautiful.

Cheap Vacations

The resistance of the workers to 'flowerpot socialism' carried over at first to *Kraft durch Freude* or KdF. The scheme was copied from the Italian Fascist system of *Opera Nazionale Dopolavoro* established as early as 1925. Its aim was to create a leisure culture for the workers, a culture that was not independent of the factory or *Volksgemeinschaft*. KdF was divided into four main departments—after hours entertainment, mass tourism, sport and night classes. Quickly KdF emerged as the most popular element in the German Labour Front, and while it may not have seduced every German worker it did conjure up a new world of opportunities. Workers were told that National Socialism, more than the encrusted Wilhelmine structures [those of Emperor Wilhelm II] or the chaos of [the] Weimar [democracy], offered social mobility, the chance of improvement. And it offered physical mobility, the opportunity to travel, often for the first time, to Bavaria or the Black Forest. By 1935 the first worker cruises were being advertised to Madeira or the Norwegian fjords. Very swiftly KdF developed into the first modern mass package tourism concern, with 880 million Reichsmark earmarked between 1934 and 1942 to subsidize tourism. A three-day tour to admire the blossoming gardens around Lake Constance was offered for 7,90 Reichsmark, including train travel from Munich, lunch and a boat ticket. A seven-day Christmas break in the Black Forest was 34 Reichsmark, all inclusive. The annexation of Austria in 1938 yielded yet more possibilities for travel to the Tirol, to Salzburg and to Carinthia. Mussolini's Italy was ready to provide a link up between state travel companies and ordinary Germans discovered Lake Garda, which has remained a popular destination for German tourists. . . .

Women Lived with Illusions of Motherhood and Freedom

Women were the first to spot the yawning chasm between the myth of the perfect Aryan, blonde, soft, baby-producing German mother and the wartime reality of food and soap shortages. There was a revolutionary potential in women but it was never tapped. Women barely figure in the annals of the

German resistance, the most prominent exceptions being the Munich student Sophie Scholl, executed for distributing an anti-Nazi leaflet and Mildred Harnack of the Red Orchestra, also executed. The few brave women who sheltered Jews are heavily outnumbered by the hordes of female denouncers. The fundamental point is that women found enough in the regime to satisfy them, that the Nazis for all their apparent misunderstanding and manipulation of the female sex discovered ways of keeping women out of the political arena or upholding their loyalty to the Führer. The theme of our essay . . . is the exercise of choice in a dictatorship. Germans do not deny they were seduced by Hitler for the seduction of the nation is such a broad brush concept that it diminishes personal responsibility; they gave way to the Führer in a momentary lapse, the Führer was 'irresistible'. But our intent is to examine how in detail this seductive process worked: which policy, which manoeuvre dulled the senses of which section of society. One has to search for explanations why people do not act against tyranny. . . .

The single mothers were pampered, the children treated like infant heroes.

National Socialism found a way of combining its motherhood ideology with the illusion of emancipation; those looking for a way out of the tight corset of pre-First World War German motherhood could still find something of what they wanted within the Nazi repertoire. Indeed, some German women still look back to the Third Reich as the best time of their lives.

Eva Sternheim-Peters, a member of the Nazi Bund Deutsche Mädel, BDM, (League of German Girls) recalls in her memoirs, published in 1987, that 'in the forty years since the end of the Hitler dictatorship I have never felt so intensely, never functioned as such a free, politically aware creature, never had such political responsibility.' She was not writing as a dyed-in-the-wool National Socialist but rather as someone who was given early managerial power of a kind not previously (and indeed not subsequently) accorded to women. As a 16-year-old girl Sternheim-Peters was responsible—without adult supervision—for the organization of a Jung Maedel camp, a collection of over a hundred primary school-aged children. She organized the daily routine, arranged parents' evenings, musical and theatre performances, parties and expeditions. It was then that she realized that 'when it came down to it women can do as much as men'. Other BDM activists make similar comments: 'It was then that I developed into an independent person.'

Ideology and Reality

All this happened in spite of rather than because of a Nazi programme. The Nazi system on the surface seemed to emphasize the role differences between men and women, with women firmly confined to the kitchen and the bedroom. The reality however was that differences merged. . . .

Neither Hitler nor the Nazis were much interested in furthering or helping the cause of women. But they did aim to break up the family in the conventional sense even as they simultaneously preached traditional family values. This helped almost by accident to liberate women. . . .

Hollow Assurances of Liberation

Emancipation put gender differences at the core of society, the Nazis insisted that race was the nub of it all, the solidarity of shared blood overrode sexual differentiation. It was therefore determined to roll back advances made in the 1920s while at the same time giving the impression that women were freer than ever before. The rollback actually began before the arrival of National Socialism. The male majority in the Reichstag ensured that the savings in the civil service, prompted by the inflation of 1923, were made at the expense of married women who were dismissed from their posts. Even the Social Democrats argued in 1932 that only single women should work as civil servants. No women's organization at the time registered a protest—they, and women as a whole, were ready to make common cause with the Nazis.

Motherhood—on this there was no dispute and little fluctuation in policy—was the cornerstone of social and racial policy. From 1935 abortion was made legal but only for the 'racially inferior'—Roma, forced labourers and from 1938 Jewish women. The sterilization of the mentally and physically handicapped, begun already in 1933, was also part of this philosophy. By 1945 half a million people had been sterilized. The Nazi plan was that only 'racially valuable' women should give birth but 20–30 per cent of the German population did not meet the Nazi criteria of racial hygiene. The abortion trade boomed; racially 'pure' Germans were forbidden to terminate their pregnancies at the risk of imprisonment. Newspapers were full of accounts of trials of gynaecologists who had disposed of unwanted but racially acceptable pregnancies. The doctors faced the death sentence. Access to condoms was restricted to soldiers at the front; advertisements for contraceptives were banned. Sexual advice centres were shut down.

The Nazis used not only repressive means to boost the birth rates but also bribes. From October 1935 those wanting to marry had to secure a health certificate; no registry office could carry out a wedding without this document. But once certificates were signed the couple qualified for shopping credit vouchers to the value of RM 1000 (the average annual salary in 1933 was around RM1520). If the couple had four children the debt was written off. The Mother's Day holiday was made into a red-letter day. Fecund mothers of Aryan children were awarded the Mother's Cross (Bronze) for four to six children, Silver for six to eight and Gold for nine or more. On Mother's Day 1939, three million women were awarded medals for their exceptional achievements in bringing forth children. The birth rate rose: 20.4 live births for every 1000 inhabitants in 1939, 5 points higher than in 1932 and almost the peak level of 1924. In this way motherhood became a political duty and responsibility. Hitler spoke of a 'battle with existential importance for our people'. Motherhood was no longer private but rather a contribution to the racial war against inferior peoples. Sex, too, began to lose its private dimension. If sex is for reproduction and reproduction serves the nation then attitudes about marriage and extramarital relations also have to change. The incentive to many was financial and in areas where the Catholic church still exercised some influence, traditional. But the stigma of illegitimacy, the prejudices against single motherhood, crumbled. The Lebensborn programme—to breed a master race—made something of an honour out of illegitimacy. The single mothers were pampered, the children treated like infant heroes. 'Not every woman can get a husband but every woman can be a mother' was a slogan propagated by Nazis woman league chief Gertrud Scholtz-Klink.

4

Hitler's Powerful Memory Created the Illusion of Genius

Edleff H. Schwaab

In this selection, drawn from his book *Hitler's Mind: A Plunge into Madness*, psychologist Edleff H. Schwaab focuses on the nature of Hitler's intellect and how it helped him come to power. According to Schwaab, Hitler's memory was extremely powerful, and his ability to recount a broad range of facts and details intimidated those around him and gave them a sense that he was a genius. Furthermore, Schwaab says, Hitler himself believed that he was intellectually gifted and he thus viewed himself as one of the great figures of history and thereby deserving of universal admiration. Consequently, Schwaab argues, few were willing to question Hitler's authority or judgment, and Hitler was unwilling to tolerate any such differences of opinion. Although he grants that Hitler had some clear talents, Schwaab maintains that Hitler was neither a genius nor a true intellectual, given that he lacked the ability to think critically and to weigh facts and arguments fairly. As Schwaab sees it, Hitler insisted on selectively filtering the knowledge he acquired so that his dangerous and mistaken worldview was never challenged. Furthermore, his anti-intellectualism appealed to the masses, Schwaab says, who tended to blame the turmoil of the 1920s on intellectuals and the educated elites.

Hitler spoke at huge beer hall rallies with chilling effectiveness, and in all personal contacts he controlled

Edleff H. Schwaab, *Hitler's Mind: A Plunge into Madness*. New York: Praeger, 1992. Copyright © 1992 by Edleff H. Schwaab. Reproduced by permission of Greenwood Publishing Group, Inc., Westport, CT.

conversations with commanding rigor. None of his follow-ers thought of him, in terms of modern concepts in the field of psychiatry, as a disturbed individual obsessed with para-noid notions. To the contrary, most Germans saw in him a genius with a brilliant grasp of global issues and a clairvoy-ant vision of what the future would hold for them. Some-how Hitler saw to it that he gained such a reputation. Be-hind the image and the gift of tirades lay his mesmerizing oratory, his iron will, and, above all, his missionary zeal.

A glance at these qualities provides us with a partial an-swer to questions about how his mental abilities enabled him to cause his collaborators and the masses of the people to perceive him as an extraordinary individual. An analysis of his mode of thinking and reasoning, as well as of the complexities and adaptability of the content of his thoughts, should help us gain a better understanding of the nature of the workings of his mind.

The Illusion of Genius

In the absence of any formal education or any display of ex-ceptional artistic talent and of any outstanding intellectual accomplishments, nothing served Hitler better than his ex-traordinary memory in creating the illusion of his being some kind of genius. He did not tell us how he acquired his vast fund of factual information, except for saying he read a lot. But everyone who knew him was impressed by the skill with which he utilized his knowledge. He was able to retain and readily recall an unusually wide range of facts, certainly more than any ordinary mortal would care to remember.

His retentive memory often obscured the trivial nature of what he had rendered to memory. For instance, thirty years later he still recalled the make and serial number of a bicycle he rode during the First World War in 1915, and he astonished his listeners with his command of an incredible amount of technical detail of military weaponry, such as data on every major vessel in the German and British navies—their power plants, armor plating, and gun displacements, for example. When the chief of staff, Wilhelm Keitel, cited ammunition expenditures during the French campaign in the summer of 1940, Hitler countered by comparing these figures with the consumption of 210 mm and 150 mm am-munition during the year 1916, and doing so by quoting monthly figures.

One of his faithful secretaries was so flabbergasted, she reported after the war, that "I often asked myself how one human being could preserve so many facts." His entire staff complained about being browbeaten and felt "discouraged by the feeling that, since the Führer [leader] had already thought of everything himself, there was little they could contribute by way of suggestions or initiatives," so [historian] David Irving tells us.

By employing his peculiar practice of making people feel inferior, Hitler deliberately surrounded himself with the illusion that he was all-knowing. The eloquence of his informed arguments was simply intimidating and fostered the image of an exceptional mind at work. If his gift to attain astonishing technical details of weapons systems and design of armament of any kind used by German and foreign armies is judged to be a critical dimension of superior intelligence, Hitler must be said to have been a brilliant man. Similarly, if the ability to organize and control a well-functioning political system and initiate the building of the biggest war machine in Europe within an incredibly short time span and if the grasp of military matters and strategic imagination displayed during the years prior to his disastrous Russian campaign are any indications of unusual mental powers, Hitler again can be said to have stood head and shoulders above anyone in the circle of leaders of the Third Reich. Are these observations sufficient to call him a brilliant person? . . .

Hitler's Intellect

Hitler's exceptional memory proved one of the strongest and readily identifiable features of his intelligence. But this one aspect of his mind is not sufficient to call him a genius. The nature of his memory functions, though, permits us to make a limited number of important inferences and provides us with a broader perspective of the overall picture of his intelligence.

First of all, the amount of knowledge Hitler was able to accumulate cannot be separated from his ability to learn. It would be a mistake to view his school failure as an indication of intellectual limitations when it was essentially the result of both the intractable quality of his mind and his self-reliance on learning only on his own terms. Without the retention of the extensive reading material and the ability to master a style of constant recitation of information in his dealings with people, he could not have succeeded in acquiring skills in engaging in complex social behavior. His superb memory had always been an essential part of his mentality since his childhood and was not a later acquisition.

By employing his peculiar practice of making people feel inferior, Hitler deliberately surrounded himself with the illusion that he was all-knowing.

Second, in the process of loading his mind with facts, Hitler developed the habit of screening out whatever did not fit into the framework of his ideas. Feeling compelled to be selective in absorbing anything he read, he aimed at achieving closure as soon as possible to stop the agony of thought confusion and prevent flooding his mind with complex and unrelated elements of knowledge. He had to protect himself from experiencing the awful prospect of having to change his views. His mind worked incessantly to find an outline or scheme or thought system that enabled him to classify information and place his facts into a larger context of ideas. Eventually, a *Weltanschauung* [world view] emerged with world-spanning visions and religiouslike dogmas to generate a sense of clarity in the flow of his thoughts about politics and policies, Jews and Germans, racial superiority and inferiority, nationhood and society, and human nature and the meaning of human existence itself. The obsessional drive to make all facts manageable and sensible in their relationship to each other allowed him to maintain inner balance. He had to make sure of his choices in selecting what information should penetrate his consciousness.

Third, a person with an insatiable appetite to know facts does not make a thinker. In spite of his self-image of holding profound and prophetic thoughts, Hitler was a man who sustained himself intellectually by clinging tenaciously to a personal frame of reference—his ideology. In the firm belief his ideas were original, he saw no need to acknowledge the sources of his information, nor any need to quote authors or discuss any books he had read. He meant to protect himself from being found out. [Historian] Werner Maser spoke of

Hitler's fearfulness that in the "unlikely event of being mistaken, his authority would be undermined." Through the instant recall of facts and knowledge and their clever use in boosting his arguments, Hitler succeeded in perpetuating the impression among those who listened to him that he was omniscient.

Fourth, to make any concessions or work toward a compromise or modify or discard old conceptions was unacceptable to Hitler. It would have been self-betrayal. He could not possibly deviate from all he had worked for so desperately: achieving closure. Eventually, he felt sure he had reached a point where he could declare that he had built a "granite foundation" on which to rest his entire world view. What he had experienced emotionally to be real had shaped his basic understanding of reality. When pridefully speaking of a "granite foundation" for all his thoughts, he accurately described the condition of a mind closed to any new insights.

Finally, Hitler claimed to have been inspired by some higher kind of providential guidance. Dreading to be perceived as an ordinary human being, he lifted himself above the level of the common politician whose basic tactics of winning a voting advantage he held in utter contempt. Hitler aimed high. He declared, "What will have to be proclaimed is a new view of the world, not just a new election slogan.". . .

Longing for Greatness

Hitler's craving to be recognized as a thinker of the first order was fed by an extraordinary sense of narcissistic entitlement. The productions of his mind cannot be mistaken for intellectual brilliance, the admirable and most envied human asset attributed to highly educated people who have made an exceptional contribution to the development of culture, science, and society. Hitler's exaggerated sense of self-importance allowed him to rank himself among such outstanding people, and he sought desperately to find universal recognition. His claim to greatness in the end failed because he was unable to make any kind of enduring contribution to the social well-being of people. He accomplished nothing to cause him to be viewed as a person with exceptional intellectual gifts. All his mental energies were directed toward forming and hanging on rigidly to a set of ideas that proved to have horrifying consequences for humankind.

At no time did Hitler show the curiosity of an intellectual who carefully weighs information before adopting it for future use. He did not care about any intellectual matters, except in a most superficial sense, and he never tried to engage in a scholarly dialogue to find a mature intellectual orientation to sort out the flood of his expansive thoughts and ideas. With the pretentiousness of a person who has answers but no questions, he built a pseudo-intellectual world for himself in which he avoided incoherence by trusting only his own judgments in acquiring knowledge. His memory functioned without discriminating clearly between soft and hard knowledge; even rumors and subjective observations he accepted as factual information. Relying blindly on the validity of his own conclusions, he became the antithesis of a true intellectual. The superb memory of his untutored mind could not make him one.

Hitler had despised educated people ever since his school days. Max Domarus [a Nazi archivist] tells us that "he was disgusted by intellectuals. He pursued them with sarcasm and derided their human weaknesses, their arrogance, and critical inclinations." Hitler regarded Germany's intellectuals as "self-isolating and ossified individuals who have lost all lively connections with the people." They had become alienated from the population, he asserted; worse, they had not distinguished themselves by showing any will power. "Germans never lacked scientific education, thank God, but they certainly lacked will power and decision-making power," he stated.

Through the instant recall of facts and knowledge and their clever use in boosting his arguments, Hitler succeeded in perpetuating the impression among those who listened to him that he was omniscient.

Hitler meant to prepare the German people for war, not for intellectual pursuits. They had to be ready, he said, for the upcoming struggle among the nations to achieve world supremacy. To accomplish this goal he needed political and military leaders, not intellectuals. He explained, "In the contest of two nations with each other . . . the one which has the best talent represented in their top leadership will emerge victorious." As far as he was concerned, Germans simply lacked the warrior mentality he tried to foster in them. Intellectuals were known only for their "pityful cowardice."

This bitter resentment toward Germany's intellectual elite had its roots in very personal feelings. When Hitler chided intellectuals for the arrogance with which "they have looked down on anyone who failed to meet obligatory school requirements," he made an obvious reference to his own dismal status as a school dropout who conveniently blamed teachers for his own failings. In anger he had ever since turned his back on the academic world, and later on he took pride in joining a political party composed of humble folks, the German Workers party. This step was "the most far-reaching decision I had made in my whole life," he said.

Appealing to the Masses

Hitler showed no hesitation in assailing his hated intellectuals publicly. As soon as he was in power, in the afternoon of the First Congress of the German Workers Union in Berlin on May 10, 1933, he shouted:

> I know their minds: constantly crafty, constantly testing, but also constantly insecure, constantly moving, in motion, never committed. Whoever wants to build a Reich on those intellectual foundations will learn that he built on sand. . . . The broad masses in the country . . . have something: they have loyalty, they have endurance, they have stability.

The skepticism of intellectuals toward his future plans enraged Hitler again and again. He called them "enemies of the people in our own country." The pervasiveness of a nearly all-consuming hatred reached a point at which he pondered exterminating all intellectuals "if we did not need them so badly." They were nothing more than "blase decadents and useless surplus goods of nature."

Were such words heard by enough Germans to alarm them about the mentality of their leader? In the confusion of the dreadful postwar conditions of a country torn by strife and civil war, a subconscious resentment toward academicians must have prevailed. They were blamed for their alleged failure to save the nation after the war and make the program of the Weimar Republic work. In these times of constant crisis, the masses of Germans were not receptive to any civil or intellectually minded leadership and did not feel offended by Hitler's anti-intellectual stance.

In a discussion of the revolutionary trend in our modern age, [the librarian of Congress] James Billington suggested that radical changes did not have their roots in social conflict in any given society but were spawned by visions of a small elite of "gifted, self-indulgent and restless intellectuals who yearned to create a perfect secular order." Hitler did not fit this mold. He certainly held utopian visions of a Thousand-Year Reich, but he was essentially a nonintellectual, spellbinding orator with a seductive vision of a better life for all Germans, who in turn failed to hear his message clearly: that this better life would be brought about at the expense of Jews. It was a most tragic moment in history when Germans did not dread the possibility of committing themselves to the leadership of a man who would twist an idea into the worst sort of tyranny.

In the last analysis, Hitler was a political and intellectual charlatan whose exceptional mind purveyed ideas draped in some kind of world view—as politicians often are apt to do—but whose disturbing delusions about the necessity to settle the fateful rivalry between Jews and Germans "by the sword" was lost on Germans among the many other ideological messages advanced at the time by Communists, Separatists, and Socialists, both of the national and international variety. In the turmoil of the times, Germans did not distinguish between anti-intellectual crackpot agitators and far-sighted political leaders. The line between these two types of leadership was lost when they failed to see that their Führer stood apart from other leaders of the country because of his brutal use of power—not because of his humanity or rationality. They trustingly relied on the propaganda portrayal of a man claiming to reason abstractly when he gave no indications of having any use for contemplation or reflection. Germany's intellectuals let down their fellow Germans by not despising the man who regarded them merely as stumbling blocks to his conception of "true" human achievement. In making the political choice in favor of Hitler, Germans failed to see that by opting to join the Nazi movement heart and soul, they opted to risk their own nationhood.

5

Hitler Established a System of Police Terror

Robert Gellately

One way that Hitler and the Nazis gained public support was by responding swiftly, and harshly, to petty crime. At first, as Robert Gellately points out, this was done by giving the police the right to arrest people preventively or to supposedly protect suspects from the mob. Then, according to Gellately, Hitler undermined, step by step, a suspect's right to a trial and the tradition of a lack of ideological or political interests among the police. Soon the police became accustomed to their new power to define the law, and Hitler's personal sentencing of one hundred suspects in June 1934 gave the public a chance to adapt to the new absence of trials, Gellately says. In the end, he notes, a private critical remark about the regime could land a person in a concentration camp. Gellately is Professor and Strassler Family Chair for the Study of Holocaust History at Clark University in Worcester, Massachusetts.

The perception that Germany was falling apart during the Great Depression was reinforced by what seemed like a crime wave. Such perceptions were fuelled by the media, but the feeling that crime was increasing was not entirely without basis, for all across Germany, there was a steady climb for most years from 1927 to 1932 in thefts of all kinds, as well as in armed robbery and fraud. The rise was continuous in large cities (with 50,000 or more inhabitants), and some crimes nearly doubled between 1927 and 1932. In the last years of the Weimar Republic, newspapers were full of stories about crime, drugs, and murder, including the activities of organized gangs. There were many accounts of finance scandals, sexual predators, serial murderers, and even cannibalism. The emergence of gays and the growth of pornography were held up as evidence of depravity. The blossoming of unconventional styles in art and music made Berlin famous and drew freedom-loving souls from all around the world, where they celebrated their emancipation. It was just this kind of 'un-German' behaviour that many good citizens despised.

Law and order stories became constituent parts of Nazi mythology and were exaggerated.

The open society and democratic freedoms were new to Germany, and many people longed nostalgically for a more disciplined society of the kind they identified in their minds with the era before 1914. Many Germans, and not just those in the conservative, religious, or Nazi camps believed that the liberal Weimar Republic was a degenerate society, and that their country was on the road to ruin.

'The Fist Comes Down!'

Christopher Isherwood, the English novelist, wrote in 1933 just before leaving the free and easy Berlin he loved in the 1920s, that the newspapers were 'becoming more and more like copies of a school magazine. There is nothing in them but new rules, new punishments, and lists of people who have been "kept in"'. Law-abiding citizens, of course, saw matters differently, and could hardly fail to be pleased that police began to take seriously their concerns about crime and loose morals. One woman fondly recalled long after the Third Reich was gone, that even during the early years of the new regime, the laws were stiffened and supposedly even thieves were shot, so that thereafter 'nobody took anything that belonged to anyone else'.

The Nazi approach to crime was not to search out its deeper social causes, but to enforce existing laws far more vigorously. The Nazi motto was summed up in a front-page story of their leading newspaper in the phrase 'the fist comes down'. They adopted this stance even before the Reichstag fire [at the site of parliament] at the end of February 1933. They appointed new Police Presidents for a number of major cities, including Berlin, where hardliners promptly declared war on crime. The impression conveyed in the press was that the Nazi Party and the German police had a lot in common, as both hated Communism and were determined to stamp out crime. . . .

'Preventive' and 'Protective' Arrests

In the early months of 1933, the police got temporary 'preventive' arrest powers to fight the Communists. These powers enabled the police to dispense with hearings before a judge and to hold Communists in what was called 'protective custody'. Until the Third Reich, protective custody was used in Germany to shield untried people from the wrath of the mob and keep them out of harm's way. Beginning in 1933, the meaning of 'protective custody' was turned on its head. It became a weapon in the hands of the Gestapo [the new political police], a euphemism for their regular arrest and confinement practices. They could pick up men and women, send them to a concentration camp without trial, and keep them there indefinitely.

The Gestapo systematized their use of 'protective custody', anchored it in the exceptional measures decree at the end of February 1933, and never looked back. The system of 'police justice' was established at the expense of citizens' legal rights, and at first it existed alongside, and to some extent in conflict with, the regular justice system. With Hitler's backing, however, police prerogatives soon got the upper hand. The Gestapo used their new powers to track widely defined political crimes, and the Kripo [German investigative police] obtained similar 'preventive arrest' powers to pursue other types of crimes.

As the 'emergency' began to fade in 1933, some of Hitler's Cabinet colleagues were ambivalent about the apparent ascendancy of the police and the sweeping arrests. However, their objections were half-hearted and in any case were directed 'against neither the principle nor the practice of protective custody as such, nor opposed to its complete arbitrariness and lawlessness'. The Ministers of Justice and Interior were unwilling or unable to control the social dynamics of the situation. Interior Minister Wilhelm Frick was more concerned about procedures, than substance, but if anything he favoured the police over Nazi Party hooligans.

Law and order stories became constituent parts of Nazi mythology and were exaggerated. Nevertheless, the police were quick to use their new powers, even against petty thieves like exploiters and swindlers, who were packed off (without trials) to concentration camps. The same thing happened to butchers and cattle dealers who took advantage of the Depression to force farmers to sell livestock at low prices. Newspapers self-righteously declared that these criminals would now 'have an opportunity to discover through manual labour, how difficult the work of a farmer is and how much sweat and work it takes in these hard times to hold on to a bit of soil'. These stories about swift justice, undoubtedly fuelled populist myths about the regime as a crime fighter, and thus earned it considerable support.

In September 1933, using imagery drawn from the military, the police declared open war on the beggars and vagrants. Citizens were discouraged from showing false pity, and asked to give their money instead to charities. A police sweep across the country picked up as many as 100,000, and as a recent study puts it, 'never before had the police in Germany taken in so many people by way of a single police action'.

Praise in the Press

In the days and weeks that followed, the press was full of glowing stories about the event, like one that proudly proclaimed 'Berlin, a City without beggars'. In December another featured a 'Report on the Cleansing of Berlin', stating that 'the measures of the Berlin police and their results find the support of everyone. The capital city is freed within a few months from an evil whose scale represented an unacceptable annoyance to Berliners and to visitors in the city.'

The beginning of better times and diminished crime was signalled in a Christmas-time story that ran under the headline, 'Insecurity Diminished: there is work again for the people; now we can go home again at night in peace.' Although some of the beggars who were arrested were soon released, the no-nonsense image of the new system was hammered home in the press. In Hamburg the police took the opportunity not only to arrest beggars, but to force unemployed single men and others to work for any welfare support they received. There was a crackdown on petty criminals, like those who lived from the avails of prostitution. On 24 November 1933, the penalty for this crime was drastically increased, from a minimum of one month (in less onerous-style prison or workhouse), to a minimum of five years in the hardest form of it.

Almost immediately after Hitler's appointment, the impression in the press was that at the very least, more use would be made of the death penalty and it would be carried out sooner after sentencing than in the past. There were also menacing announcements that capital punishment could be used for 'violations' of measures adopted by the new government. . . .

Most people accepted that Hitler (not the courts) 'sentenced' the 100 or so culprits to death.

Once Hitler's new police got a taste for speedy measures, by which they could bypass time-consuming legal procedures, there was no chance they were ever really going to dispense with them. In mid-1934 they got an opportunity to bid for public support, when they finally came down on the Storm Troopers (SA). On 30 June 1934, the leaders of the SA were killed on Hitler's orders. During this so-called 'night of the long knives' the radical ambitions of the SA, who kept longing for a real social revolution, were brought to a halt once and for all. The event was presented to the German public as an attempted coup by SA leader Ernst Röhm, but no effort was made to hide the fact that Röhm was executed without a semblance of a trial. Most people accepted that Hitler (not the courts) 'sentenced' the 100 or so culprits to death. Far from causing Germans to have second thoughts, by all accounts this first mass murder of the Third Reich paid positive political dividends for Hitler, because it gave many citizens the opportunity to accept the new 'normality' and the coercive side of the dictatorship. The police wanted the government to be more trusting than to censor news and to be upfront about what happened to those killed during the purge. They felt it was impossible to stop citizens from listening to foreign radio, and suggested it would be best to publish 'authentic explanations to remove the basis of wild rumours'.

Hitler signalled that political stabilization had arrived by granting a selective amnesty on 10 August 1934. He used the occasion of President [Paul von] Hindenburg's death and the opportunity to publicize the 'unification of the office of Reich President with that of the Reich Chancellor'. The amnesty was supposed to still the worries of top civil servants and to assure the general population that all was well, in spite of what was called the Röhm 'revolt'. According to press reports, as many as one-third of those in 'protective custody' were released in some places, and more concentration camps were dissolved. The reports stated that 'deadly enemies' who prepared and carried out acts of treason were not included in the amnesty, but that many already had left the country.

Hitler was not interested in legal niceties, so it was characteristic that he did not disband the Gestapo, nor curtail its powers, even though most of those considered real enemies were by that time already gone. On the contrary, on 20 June 1935, he gave [Heinrich] Himmler his blessing to expand the concentration camps, which had been closing down everywhere. Himmler also obtained Hitler's support on 18 October 1935 to broaden the powers of the police. A meeting between them took place shortly after the infamous Nuremberg Party rally in September at which Hitler announced discriminatory laws against the Jews.

They tried 'malicious gossip' cases and verbal attacks on the government.

The Nuremberg rally in 1935, heralded as the 'National Party Meeting of Freedom', represented a milestone in the establishment of the dictatorship's system of racial discrimination and persecution. Of three new laws passed on 15 September by the Reichstag which met in Nuremberg, the most important turned out to be the 'law for the protection of German blood and German honour'. The law forbad further marriages and extramarital sexual relations between Jews and 'Germans' and people of 'associated or similar blood'.

Another part of the Nuremberg event, one frequently overlooked, took place on 11 September, when Hitler announced by proclamation what he termed a 'struggle against the internal enemies of the nation'. These 'enemies' were vaguely defined as 'Jewish Marxism and the parliamentary democracy associated with it'; 'the politically and morally depraved Catholic Centre Party'; and 'certain elements of an unteachable, dumb and reactionary bourgeoisie'. The proclamation did not say what steps would be taken, but it sounded like the beginning of a social war. The speech was all the more curious in that it went on to underline how Germany enjoyed greater security and tranquillity than at any time in the recent past. Hitler contrasted the situation in 1935 with the 'ferment of decomposition' and 'signs of decay' that existed at the time of his appointment.

A little over a month after the Nuremberg rally, on 18 October 1935 Hitler and Himmler broadened the concepts of 'enemy' and 'crime' the new police were supposed to fight. The Gestapo was not going to vanish after all, nor were the camps. The number of camp prisoners had been falling since mid-1933, but promptly began to grow again.

By mid-1935 the new police were getting the upper hand. At this time the dictatorship had to respond to the issue of whether suspects in protective custody should be allowed legal counsel. The argument as stated by Dr Werner Best, a key figure behind the creation of the new system, was simple. The main consideration 'from the point of view of the leadership of the state', he said, was whether or not giving lawyers access to clients would help in the battle against the state's 'deadly enemies'. Lawyers' questions were inevitable, but were incompatible with the state leadership's 'trust in the organizations given the mission to defend against the attacks of enemies'. Best said that because the Gestapo regarded protective custody as its 'most important weapon' against enemies of state, any weakening of that weapon was the equivalent of strengthening the dangers threatening the state. Therefore, he concluded, no lawyers should be allowed as the usual 'procedural forms of the judiciary were totally inapplicable for the struggle against the enemies of state under the present circumstances'. That argument was met by a minor quibble from the Ministry of Justice, which was silenced when Himmler informed officials on 6 November 1935 of a Hitler order barring lawyers access to anyone held in protective custody.

The Political Police

The creation of the new Gestapo system culminated with a Prussian law of 10 February 1936. According to this law virtually any actions taken by the Gestapo were no longer subject to court review, not even in the event of wrongful arrest, and no one could sue for damages. In other words, if the Gestapo was above the law even earlier, by early 1936 that situation was formalized. Henceforth, the only route open for any complaints was to appeal to the Gestapo head office (Gestapa). Far from being hushed up, the full implications of these developments were spelled out to the public in the press, so that no doubt could exist that citizens' basic legal rights were all but ended. Gestapo headquarters in Berlin simply wished to ensure that local officials did not overuse their powers of arrest and bring discredit on the police. Although in theory the legal immunity enjoyed by the Gestapo did not apply to the rest of the police, if and when they acted on behalf of the Gestapo, what they did could not be challenged either.

The Nazis worked out a clearly articulated *völkisch* or Fascist theory of the police by the mid-1930s, and proudly presented it for the edification and enlightenment of the public. The most succinct statement of this new theory was by Werner Best, the legal expert at Gestapo headquarters. Although his remarks were published in a specialist journal, summaries of them made their way into the popular press. Germans could now read that the police powers justified initially to fight Communism had a new rationale. Best stated flatly that the new police regarded 'every attempt' to realize or to maintain any political theory besides National Socialism 'as a symptom of sickness, which threatens the healthy unity of the indivisible volk organism'. All such efforts would be 'eliminated regardless of the subjective intentions of their proponents'. He now said that the new police watched over the 'health of the German body politic', recognized 'every system of sickness', and destroyed all 'destructive cells'. He summed up the mission of the Gestapo as follows:

> The preventive police mission of a political police is to search out the enemies of state, to watch them and at the right moment to destroy them. In order to fulfil this mission the political police must be free to use every means required to achieve the necessary goal. In the National Socialist leader state it is the case, that those institutions called upon to protect state and people to carry out the will of the state, possess as of right the complete authority required to fulfil their

task, an authority that derives solely from the new conception of the state and one that requires no special legal legitimization. . . .

The Courts

The courts were the source of many more stories about the dictatorship's approach to law and order. New 'emergency' Special Courts were created by decree of 21 March 1933 in each of the twenty-six higher court districts across the country. These courts, as well as the 'malicious gossip' decree, came into force on the famous 'Day at Potsdam', and were meant by judicial officials to show that the courts could be counted on to shield the new regime from criticism. The hope was that the regime would return to the rule of law, and that these 'emergency' courts would fade away. Quite to the contrary, they became permanent, and by February 1941, there would be sixty-three of them, with some higher court districts having as many as four. They were initially responsible for trying two political offences, particularly those accused of posing a political threat to the 'people and state'—as that broad notion was embodied in the so-called Reichstag Fire Decree of 28 February 1933. They tried 'malicious gossip' cases and verbal attacks on the government. The latter was broadened further in a new law of 20 December 1934 which, among other things, made public criticism not just of the government, but of the Nazi Party, into a crime. Such a 'malicious' attack was unlawful even if the remarks were made in private, at least if it could be shown that the person responsible knew or should have known that the statements might be repeated in public.

These courts reached into the private lives of citizens, as nearly all such 'crimes' were verbal exchanges among the people, and they were discovered only when one person denounced someone they knew to the police. Some of these cases ended tragically, and might well have been thrown out except that the courts treated remarks as having been made 'in public' even when some were uttered among a small circle of friends or even privately.

Chapter 3

The World Responds

1

The Future of Germany Is Bleak Under Hitler

Nation

By the spring of 1933, Hitler had a firm grip on Germany. He was chancellor of the country, and although he failed to win an absolute majority in the March elections, he and his Nazis secured their dominant position by winning five million more votes than they had in the previous election. In an editorial published March 15 of that year, the *Nation*, a weekly newsmagazine in the United States, expresses deep concern for the future of Germany. Noting that the election results may well have been influenced by Nazi terror, the *Nation* insists that Hitler's rise to power nonetheless demonstrates that the Allied victory in World War I has failed to make the world safe for democracy. In particular, the editorial presciently argues that Hitler would have no qualms about turning to violence, rewriting the German constitution, and abolishing the Reichstag, the German parliament. The editorial predicts that life will become very difficult for Jews in Germany and that Hitler might well lead Germany into war.

B y adding no less than 5,528,000 to his previous vote, and with the aid of his Hugenberg Nationalist allies, whose vote actually decreased, Adolf Hitler is firmly established in the chancellorship and can now wreak his will upon what is left of the German Republic. [Alfred Hugenberg was the leader of the German National Worker's Party, DNAP.] He has achieved his goal, and the only redeeming feature of this disaster to the democratic and liberal movements in his

The Nation, "Hitler Wins," *The Nation*, vol. CXXXVI, March 15, 1933, p. 277.

country is that he has won the chancellorship by constitutional methods without resorting to violence. The constitution was respected in form, but as a matter of fact it was breached at many points. The terrorization of the voters, the wholesale suppression of the Socialist and Communist press, the arrest of the leading Communists, the raids upon the chief Jewish defense organizations—all these made Hitler's victory sure. Indeed, it is remarkable that in the face of this the Communist vote decreased by only 1,132,000 and the Social Democrat by but 135,000. None the less, the battle for democracy is lost. Herr Hitler will unquestionably unseat the Communists by *force majeure* and fraud, thereby obtaining the necessary two-thirds' majority to send the Reichstag home.

The World War a Failure

And so another fascist dictatorship arises, to remind Americans of the complete failure of our "victory" in the World War to achieve the ends we set ourselves. The world safe for democracy? Democracy perishes in Germany and those in control of her destiny not only represent, in part at least, the most odious forms of big-business and large-landowner control as they existed during the regime of the Kaiser, but are committed to universal military service, rearmament, and every one of the forms of militarism against which [President Woodrow] Wilson called all Americans to fight. The only thing lacking to complete the picture is the restoration of the monarchy; that that is not now in sight is largely because of the personal unpopularity of the former Kaiser and the former Crown Prince. But even without that prospect, Germany faces autocratic one-man rule modeled on that of [the dictator of Italy, Benito] Mussolini.

The battle for democracy is lost.

The road will not be easy for Hitler even after he has taken all the power into his hands. In the first place, the man himself is incompetent to lead, for he is totally ignorant of economic and financial questions. Whether he will permit himself to be guided by the reactionary hold-overs from the Von Papen and Von Schleicher Cabinets, who form a majority of his own, remains to be seen; he now represents

17,265,000 votes, and the Nationalists but 3,132,000—they actually lost 103,000 votes. He may therefore decline to let the tail wag the dog. Already the Hitler campaign has checked the upward movement in German industry. The agrarian situation is worse than ever, the last doses of high tariffs having naturally failed to bring prosperity to the farmers. If the economic tide runs again, however, in the direction of prosperity, if Hitler can find work for some unemployed, the number of whom is still mounting, he may satisfy the populace for a long time to come. But if even a year hence the economic situation of the country is no better—or is worse—it may be impossible for him to hold together the deluded masses who have looked upon him as a veritable savior. He has promised to lead them out of the wilderness, and if he does not do it, the disillusioned, desperate people

Adolf Hitler

will—if they can—turn to someone else. Such desertions he will undoubtedly try to combat by violence, by rewriting the constitution to suit his own purposes, as well as by practically abolishing the Reichstag and using all the instruments of propaganda as he did during the last campaign. That he will stay his hand is unthinkable. The very fact that he has carried the heretofore impregnable citadel of Bavaria, and that he has swept Prussia and completely dominates the Prussian Diet, will encourage him to smash democratic and representative institutions just as rapidly as he can. In the last analysis it will come down to a question whether the German people will permit themselves to be cowed or will rise against the most unprincipled demagogue yet to curse Germany.

Difficult Times for German Jews

By sheer ruthlessness and brutality even an incompetent dictator can hold himself in office a long time; that the policy of the Hitlerites will be "brutal" to the Communists and Social Democrats has been officially stated by one of Hitler's lieutenants. As for the Jews, they are profoundly to be pitied. Hitler may not actually resort to pogroms, as he and his men have promised that they would; he has yet to make good his boast that when he took office "heads would roll in the sand." But in the months, and perhaps the years, to come the Jews will live as marked persons, fearing the loss of their citizenship—also decreed by the Hitler platform—and facing persecution, prejudice, and personal violence. Leave Germany they cannot, unless permission is given to them by the government—even Switzerland has just increased its frontier guards to prevent those in terror of the Nazis from seeking that historic asylum which was so readily and happily granted to the revolutionists of 1848. As for the labor unions, they lost their opportunity to check this movement a long time ago, and they are now weakened and frightened. Altogether the spectacle of Germany is one to make the gods weep. It is, of course, at bottom due to the folly and the wickedness of the Treaty of Versailles. But this does not alter the fact that Germany has now become one of the danger spots of Europe, a source of unrest and international anxiety, and perhaps another threat of war.

2

Germany Throws Her Republic Overboard

Newsweek

Newsweek's cover story for its April 1, 1933, issue was about Hitler's rise to power. The magazine reported that with the passage of the Enabling Act, which expanded Hitler's personal power, a dictatorial empire had replaced the German republic. According to the magazine, the democratic parliament had essentially voted itself out of existence, and there had been very little opposition to its doing so. As *Newsweek* saw it, with the passage of the Enabling Act, Hitler's fourteen-year quest for power was complete, despite the fact that just ten years earlier Hitler had been at best a minor figure in Germany. The article concludes by noting with concern that since World War I, in addition to Germany, several European countries—including Italy, Spain, Poland, Russia, Turkey, and Austria—had been ruled by dictatorships.

The Third Reich had just been born. The German Republic lay dying. Adolf Hitler, who fathered the one and struck down the other, appeared triumphantly last week on a balcony of the Kroll Opera House in Berlin. There, a few minutes before, the Reichstag had made him Dictator of Germany.

The idolatrous crowd yelled, seeing him. With upflung arm he demanded silence. Quieted, they stared up at him. "The first chapter of our movement is closed," he shouted to their rapt, upraised faces. "Now we begin the second."

Newsweek, "Germany Throws Her Republic Overboard," *Newsweek*, vol. 1, April 1, 1933, pp. 3–5.

Momentous

Inside the Opera House the Deputies were dispersing after one of the most momentous sessions in German history. They knew when they assembled what they were there to do and they did it promptly, most of them because they wanted to, the rest because they had to.

The night before they convened, a Nazi statement hinted that if they did not give Hitler dictatorial powers he would take them.

The Nazis need not have worried. The Enabling Act which transformed an ex-corporal into a Dictator was passed, 441 to 94. Only Socialist Deputies voted against it. The 81 Communists were in jail or in hiding.

All during the session in the Opera House, thousands of Nazi sympathizers swarmed through surrounding streets. "Give us that Enabling Act," they roared. "Give us that Enabling Act or there will be a fire."

Before the vote was taken Hitler, in a 45-minute address, explained his Cabinet's policies. Usually he lashes himself into gesticulating, grimacing frenzy during the course of a speech. This time he spoke quietly. Approving roars came regularly from the rows of brown-shirted Deputies. As he ended, they leaped to their feet, thundered an ovation and sang "Deutschland Ueber Alles."

He had said little to make them tingle. His speech was noteworthy for only two things: His foreign policy was mild as milk. His domestic policy omitted the radical half of the radical-reactionary program on which he wooed and won the German masses.

Germany, he said, wants equality with other countries but also wants to live in peace with the world.

"Broad" and "far-seeing" he said of [Italian dictator Benito] Mussolini's new plan for a four-power peace club in Europe. He expressed good-will toward France, where his movement is anathema, and toward Austria, where himself was born 43 years ago, the son of a customs official, and where a dictatorship has been established to keep National Socialism down.

He hoped for cordial relations with the Vatican, though Catholic leaders in Germany have condemned him, and with Soviet Russia, though his onslaught against Communists makes Moscow boil.

Germany, he said, wants equality with other countries but also wants to live in peace with the world. She does not wish to increase her armaments unless other nations refuse to reduce theirs.

Indiscussable

One of his domestic policies, he declared, would be to "extirpate communism." Another would be to put the unemployed to work and to save the impoverished farmers. Still others would be to promote private business initiative, avoid currency experiments, and purify the body politic morally. At present, his Cabinet "regards the question of monarchic restoration as indiscussable."

[The Reichstag] scrapped parliamentary democracy.

The rights of Catholics and Protestants, he said, would not be touched. As for the rights of Jews, he vaguely but menacingly remarked that his Cabinet "could not tolerate that adherence to a certain confession or membership in a certain race should be construed as a dispensation from lawful obligations, let alone a license to commit or tolerate crimes."

Determined

His calm forsook him but once. Across the street from the Kroll Opera House stands the Reichstag Building, hollowed by fire just before the Mar. 5 general elections. Hitler flared as he mentioned foreign insinuations that the Nazis may have set the fire themselves. These, he said, strengthened his determination to "avenge this crime by the public execution of the incendiary and his accomplices."

Closing, he warned the opposition that his Cabinet sought its cooperation but was prepared to strangle resistance. "Now, gentlemen," he said, aiming his words at the Catholics, whose votes were needed to pass the Enabling Act, "decide on peace or war."

They decided on peace. The hall hushed portentously as Monsignor Ludwig Kaas, Catholic Centrist leader, rose from his seat. The tension eased as he read a statement indicating that the necessary two-thirds majority was won.

The Third Reich of Hitler's harangues is now an actuality.

"In view of the storm clouds in and about Germany," he read, "the Center party offers its hand to all its former foes . . . After the satisfactory objective statements of the Chancellor, the Center party can swallow a number of its important scruples and gives its consent to the Enabling Act."

The task of voicing the Socialist protest fell to the veteran Otto Wels. His speech was less challenge than supplication. The Enabling Act, he said, was unnecessary. After its victory at the polls, the Hitler government could rule constitutionally if it wished.

Raging

"Take our liberty, take our lives, but leave us our honor," he pleaded. "If you really want social reconstruction, you would need no such law as this."

Raging, Hitler sprang upright. "You're too late," he shouted at the Socialists. "We don't need you any longer in molding the fate of our nation."

Vainly Socialist Deputies sought to interrupt his tirade. Capt. Hermann Wilhelm Goering, belligerent Nazi Speaker of the Reichstag, disregarded them. "Now you listen," he would cry, and listen, perforce, they did.

Scrapped

With no more opposition than this the Reichstag passed the Enabling Act, entitled "A law for the elimination of distress from people and country." So doing, it scrapped parliamentary democracy, surrendering its powers and the people's powers to a Cabinet opposed by nearly half of the electorate on Mar. 5.

Thus Hitler's fourteen-year struggle for power ended in epochal victory. Five years ago, in the general election of May 1928, his National Socialist German Labor party won only twelve seats in the Reichstag and 800,000 popular votes. Now, with 17,500,000 popular and 288 Reichstag votes, it dominates all Germany.

Transition

Ten years ago Hitler was a clownish figure in the opera bouffe Munich beer putsch of November, 1923. Now he sits in the Chancellery in the Wilhelmstrasse and lords it over President von Hindenburg himself. The depression, which rallied discouraged recruits round his banner, and the peace treaties, which prepared them for his chauvinistic message, have had no more striking result.

Hereafter, for the next four years, the Hitler government to enact a law will have simply to promulgate it. The signature of the President will be unnecessary. Except on a few specified subjects, it can override the Constitution at will. As for the Reichstag, it has voted itself into oblivion, though Hitler indicates that he may recall it occasionally to hear it say "Amen."

There are only two small flies in the Chancellor's ointment. Theoretically, his is still a coalition Cabinet, and it is taken for granted that the Nationalist members will strive to shape his course. Theoretically, again, he can be dismissed, as he was appointed, by President von Hindenburg.

Blessing

But as a practical matter the President has given the Nazis his blessing. Furthermore, it is no longer clear that he could expel them from power even if he would.

Thus the Third Reich of Hitler's harangues is now an actuality. Field Marshal Paul von Beneckendorff und von Hindenburg has lived to see its birth, as he saw the birth of modern Germany.

Born in 1847, he was a 23-year-old lieutenant when, in 1871, the German Empire was established with a Hohenzollern, King Wilhelm of Prussia, as Emperor. He was 71, with his World War record behind him, when Wilhelm's grandson, Wilhelm II, now an exile at Doorn, announced his sensational abdication.

Liberal

Seven years later von Hindenburg himself was elected to the Presidency, to which he was re-elected last year. Meanwhile, Germany had been proclaimed a republic, the ruling houses had toppled, a National Assembly had been chosen and, meeting at Weimar in 1919, had made Friedrich Ebert President and adopted a liberal Constitution.

It is this Constitution that Hitler will override as he pleases. It was this republican Germany that died on Mar. 23 when the Reichstag passed the Enabling Act, adding Adolf Hitler to the list of Europe's post-war dictators.

Dictators

The list is now a long one. Dictatorships since the war have been common as thrones before it. Monarchies and republics alike have crumbled before their march.

• In Italy, Benito Mussolini took office in October, 1922, following his march on Rome, and four years later all parties but the Fascists had been suppressed.

• In Spain, Gen. Primo de Rivera, with a show of military might, became dictator in September, 1923, and held on until January, 1930. Spain is now thought to be heading toward dictatorship again.

• In Poland, Marshal Joseph Pilsudski seized power in 1926 and has retained it more or less openly ever since.

• In Russia, Joseph Stalin, theoretically no more than Secretary-General of the Communist party's Central Committee, is nevertheless recognized as ruler of the nation.

• In Turkey, Gazi Mustafa Kemal Pasha, President since 1923, has been boss for the same period and his People's party, of which he is sole spokesman, is the only one permitted.

• In Yugoslavia, King Alexander I abolished the Constitution in January, 1929, and ruled arbitrarily until he promulgated a new one in September, 1931.

• In Austria, Chancellor Engelbert Dollfuss assumed dictatorial powers on March 4, 1933, ruthlessly suspending constitutional rights.

• Other European countries which have tasted admitted or disguised dictatorships in the post-war period include Albania under King Zog I, Hungary under Regent Nicholas Horthy von Nagybanya, Portugal under President-General Antonio Oscar de Fragoso Carmona, Rumania under Jon Bratianu, and Greece under Prime Minister Eleutherios Venizelos.

3

Germans Have Abandoned Their Critical Faculty

Norman Angell

In the following selection, Norman Angell argues that Hitler won power not by force but by persuasion. As he sees it, there is no way Hitler and his immediate group of Nazi insiders could have overpowered tens of millions of Germans. Instead, he insists, Hitler was successful because he was able to persuade the German people to follow him by tapping into their desires. Angell believes that the Germans were ultimately responsible for bringing Hitler to power by surrendering their critical faculties and following him despite knowing his destructive intentions. According to Angell, the goal should be to persuade or reeducate them rather than to punish them. Norman Angell was a journalist and writer who earned the Nobel Peace Prize in 1933. He was a member of the Executive Committee of the League of Nations and of the British National Peace Council.

We talk of Hitler's power being based on force, terror, torture. But he did not win his power by force. He won it by persuasion, by a moral hold over the minds of millions of German folk. Let us remember that the Nazi party began as a party of thirteen members in a Bavarian beer hall, and possessed no "force," no material power at all.

How did it become a party of as many millions, come to poll thirteen millions, even before Hitler had become

Norman Angell, *For What Do We Fight?* New York: Harper & Brothers, 1939. Copyright © 1939 by Harper & Brothers. Reproduced by permission.

Chancellor? Because thirteen persons were able to impose themselves by "force" upon sixty million? The idea is, on its face, absurd. Those thirteen, or that one, could only conquer by capturing the minds of the millions; by a process of spiritual conversion. Hitler owes his power to the fact that he was able to achieve that spiritual conversion. And even if we take the view that he was the tool of vested interests, capitalist or other, the power that he won for them was achieved by getting at the minds of the millions. The pictures that we commonly draw of the Tyrant as an individual or a little coterie of a few dozen "holding down" millions by force is in truth false for the force by which the people are held down is in fact force supplied by themselves.

Those thirteen, or that one, could only conquer by . . . a process of spiritual conversion.

If you think that a man becomes dictator by the mere fact of proclaiming himself one, you can put it to very simple test. Go into the street and shout, "I am dictator of Great Britain. Obey me." What would happen? The ambulance would come along, and that would be the end of your political experiment. But if, when a mob is surging down the street, a mob full of enthusiasm or spiritual exaltation, or vindicative hate, you say with the famous Frenchman, "I must follow them, for I am their leader," and you can then go into the street and capture their minds by shouting their feelings and ideas more loudly, more strikingly than others, then you may become their dictator and they may obey you. But you will have done it by reaching their mind to an uncommon degree.

The root of it all is the mind of the common man, and the question we have to ask is how it comes that millions of people, very like ourselves, just as educated, having had for the most part schooling during more years than English folk usually have, have put Hitler in power? A French writer has pointed out that "Even though Hitler never obtained for his party alone an absolute majority in a free poll, he came to power by constitutional means, supported by a coalition of Chauvinist parties which all had been freely elected by the German people; he had obtained at the presidential election of 1932, more than 13,000,000 votes, and his party was by that time the strongest in the Reichstag. Hitler's doctrine of violence and oppression, his bestial racialism, his glorification of war (in *Mein Kampf* he wrote black on white that the war of 1914 had been wished by the whole German people) have been preached in public from the outset, in millions of books, tracts, speeches. Hitler rose to power on the promise of a war of conquest. The German people were fully informed of their leader's intentions and sacrificed their freedom with their own hands."

Persuasion Instead of Punishment

We rightly distinguish between the German people and the German government, because while you can get rid of a government or a regime, you cannot get rid of a people. We can admit that the German people are responsible for their government without either hating the people (we, too, have been responsible for bad governments), or concluding that it is practicable or desirable to "punish" them. They have become obsessed by an erroneous but sincerely held doctrine, calling, not for punishment, but conversion to a better doctrine. We can best achieve that conversion by persuading them that our doctrine of international co-operation on equal terms will give them a happier future than their present policy possibly can.

Their main fault has been to surrender their critical faculty.

Their intellectual servility to "leadership" is such that they can be led to bestial cruelty, back to some of the worst phases of the Dark Ages. The essence of their fault is that they have surrendered personal responsibility for the policy followed by their nation.

Hitler rose to power on the promise of a war of conquest.

They are not different in the character of their blood or grey matter from ourselves. We must not make Hitler's racial mistake. Their muscular tissues, their glands and physical processes are exactly as ours; the material of their brains the same. But by this surrender of personal responsibility, this intellectual abasement, they have drifted from one error to another, errors from which all their learning,

Hitler persuaded millions of Germans to surrender their critical faculties, and unquestioningly follow his leadership.

all their erudition, all their externally imposed discipline has failed to save them. . . .

Ideological Changes from One Day to the Next

How deep is the moral confusion in the minds of the belligerent peoples is revealed by what is perhaps the most amazing of all the features of the amazing history of 1939, namely, the ease with which the ideologies of whole nations can be turned completely upside down from one day to another; the way in which the loathsome heresy of Monday can become a quite readily accepted orthodoxy on Tuesday. For years, ever since the foundation of the German National Socialist Party, Bolshevism has been proclaimed by the Nazis as a foul moral pestilence, incompatible with human decency, with which no German should ever have contact. The destruction of Bolshevism was proclaimed as a sacred duty of the German people. For Germany to come to terms with it, still more to come to any sort of co-operation or alliance with it (this is one of the repeated warnings of *Mein Kampf*) would mean the destruction of the Fatherland. Yet, on a given day, without warning, the Führer [the leader, Hitler] announced that he had come to what amounts in fact to an alliance with this moral pestilence: Bolshevist Russia and Nazi Germany have proclaimed deep friendship. Nothing, it is declared, shall henceforth separate them.

The ideologies of whole nations can be turned completely upside down from one day to another.

The years of indoctrination to the effect that such a union would be against nature, morally revolting, ending in the deserved destruction of Germany, do not seem to have mattered in the least. The docile seventy millions accepted the new doctrine as readily as they had accepted the old. . . .

The spectacle that should disturb us is this: two great peoples, one of them always regarded as the most educated, scholastically most drilled, the most academic and learned of all the world, so conditioned morally and intellectually that they could acquiesce in the complete overturn from one day to another, of a faith held, up till then, with passion; so that, what was right on Monday becomes wrong on Tuesday, and wrong on Tuesday right on Wednesday. It is the measure of the moral chaos of our time.

These somersaults are inexplicable save on one ground: that there is no reasoned conviction underlying these ideologies at all on the part of the great masses. The doctrines have come to represent either sheer intellectual confusion, or a servile acquiescence in the intellectual and moral leadership of violent-minded men, a puppet-like reaction to emotional appeal, a willingness to "think with your blood"; which is not thought at all.

4

Hitler Has to Be Fought from Within Germany

George Douglas Howard Cole

George Douglas Howard Cole, writing in 1939, argues that in order to overcome Hitler and Nazism it is not enough to merely defeat Germany in war. Instead, he believes, the true goal ought to be to persuade Germans that Hitler is not the hero they take him to be. He claims that it was partly the fault of the Allies that the Germans came to follow Hitler, for they defeated Germany in World War I but did nothing to help the country re-establish itself in the international community. Cole therefore thinks it is insufficient to wage war against the Germans in order to beat Hitler. Instead, he claims, the Allies should strive to change the conditions that made Germans turn to Hitler in the first place, and encourage them to start a revolution from within. Cole was a political writer in Great Britain.

A t the end of the last war, when the actual fighting was over, the Allied Governments committed the disastrous crime and blunder of continuing to make war upon the German people. Out of that crime, aggravating the humiliations of defeat and enforced confession of "war-guilt", sprang Hitlerism—an insane parody of that Prussian militarism which we lost our chance of destroying for good and all. If, in 1918 and 1919, we had helped the German Revolution to full success; if thereafter we had promptly admitted Germany to full partnership in the League of Nations and to a friendship in which victors and vanquished could have forgotten the past in a common effort to build a better

George Douglas Howard Cole, *War Aims*. London: The New Statesman and Nation, 1939. Copyright © 1939 by The New Statesman and Nation. Reproduced by permission.

world; if we had given up promptly the senseless attempt to exact Reparations which could only be paid by the contracting of fresh debts; if we had concerted real measures of disarmament, and accompanied them by a real attempt to build up a system of European economic co-operation—if we had done these things, Hitler would have gone down to history as an unsuccessful shady adventurer, and Great Britain and France would not be to-day involved in another, and a more horrible, war. . . .

I mention our past errors . . . not out of any wish to extenuate Hitler's crimes—for I regard him as a criminal lunatic whose secure shutting-up is imperative if any shred of our civilisation is to be saved—but because I am convinced that the bringing of this war to a conclusion that will be anything other than a disaster to the whole world depends on a clear recognition of our mistakes. Hitler is, no doubt, a much greater sinner than any of our statesmen, if you judge him by his deeds. But he has, and they have not, the excuse of being out of his mind. There can be no lasting peace with Hitler, because he thinks he is God, and above all human morality. But equally there can be no decent peace made by our own statesmen, and no imaginative conduct of the war on the vital front of "intellectual operations", unless they realise and admit what they have done amiss. To put the same point quite bluntly, our propaganda will never get across to the Americans unless we show plainly by our actions that we are setting out to build a new world very different from the world of Versailles.

If we had done these things, Hitler would have gone down to history as an unsuccessful shady adventurer.

One part of this vital task of understanding is to understand Germany—its rulers, its methods, and its people as well as the régime which dominates them to-day. It is our declared war aim to dethrone Hitler and to crush Nazism as the enemy of civilised living. Good! That aim is sound, provided that we understand its implications aright. To do this involves, first and foremost, a distinction between the German people and their Nazi rulers. The Government, in dropping leaflets instead of bombs on German cities, is rightly making that distinction; and for my part I hope earnestly that, even if the Nazis start dropping bombs on us, we shall not retaliate by bombing the cities of Germany. To do so would be to identify the German people with the Nazis, and to make our declared war aim a thing of no meaning. For, though we can compass the destruction of Nazism, we can by no means set out to destroy Germany or the German people. Indeed, *we* cannot destroy Nazism by force of arms; we can only help the German people to destroy it themselves. For that supreme reason, it is vital that the distinction between Nazism and Germany shall be continually uppermost in our minds.

A Distinction Between Germans and Nazis

This distinction can, however, easily be misunderstood. It is not in Germany, as it is in Czechoslovakia and increasingly in Austria, a simple case of a peace-loving people oppressed by a set of tyrannical rulers. The German people is not burning to rise and throw off the Nazi yoke. Hitler is not merely a hated tyrant, shielded only by a mercenary bodyguard from the vengeance of the people. He is also, in a sense which we must never forget, a national hero. And since this heroic stature of his in the eyes of very many Germans is mainly the consequence of our own errors and misdeeds, we cannot afford to regard these errors and misdeeds as simply wiped out by the fact of war. Hitler menaces us today, a demon of our own making, the Frankenstein monster of our own incompetence and folly. If we are to unmake Hitler, we must take away the stuff of which such factitious heroes are made. We must recapture from the hands of the German people the distorting-mirror that we gave them— that caused so many of them to see him as hero, and not as the twisted lunatic that he really is.

The mass of the German people is not against Hitler today. Discontent there is, widespread and deep. How could there not be, in view of the ruthless regimentation, the suppression of all expression of critical opinion, the beating down of the standard of life in order to concentrate every possible effort on preparation for war? But all the evidence goes to show that, at all events among the younger Germans, there is no mass-opposition to the Nazi regime— much less to Hitler himself. Our problem in Germany is not that of releasing revolutionary forces which exist already, under the surface, and will burst forth of their own accord, as soon as the pressure of the Nazi administration is for any reason relaxed. There are no doubt groups, scattered and divided by the repression, which are only waiting for a signal of hope to break into open revolt. There is also, in the Czech and Slovak "Protectorates" and to a considerable extent in Austria—to say nothing of Poland—a real will to rebel against the tyranny to which they are subject. But it is a great mistake to suppose that the majority, or any large minority, of the German people is at present behind these secret nuclei of revolution. The main body of Germans, even though they grumble at the ceaseless exactions of the tax-gatherer, at the shortage of necessary goods, and at the continual regimentation which the Nazi system requires, nevertheless regard Hitler as the restorer of Germany's prestige among the nations, and look upon him as a leader standing above the resentments caused by the workings of the régime. After all, whatever the people have had to suffer, Hitler's *coups* have come off; and up to the present he has enjoyed in ever-increasing measure the prestige of success. The victories have been his, and they have been victories for a Germany smarting under a sense of national humiliation. The things done amiss have been put down to the minor jacks-in-office. It is quite possible for a German to dislike the Gestapo intensely, and yet to venerate Hitler as embodying the renascence of German greatness.

Nor must we forget that there is in present-day Germany no rallying point for the forces of discontent. The Nazis have succeeded in sweeping the board clear of opponents; there is no person or party against them—nowadays, not even the Communists—capable of commanding respect. If the forces of revolt do develop, they will have to find totally new leaders, and to build a new organisation up from the very foundations. It cannot be easy to stir up the German people against the Nazi regime, because the Nazi leaders have been thorough in tearing out the very heart of every potential opposition movement.

Encouraging a German Revolution

Nevertheless, we must work for a German revolution, because nothing else will make possible a happy issue out of the war. A Franco-British victory over Germany, unaccompanied by a change of attitude inside Germany, would probably lead to another Versailles—or even, perhaps, to a futile attempt to dismember the country in the hope of preventing the eighty million Germans from acting in Europe as a united force. If this were attempted, the only possible result would be a second Hitlerism worse than the first. Dismemberment of the German nation is impracticable, as well as unjust. There will be no secure peace in Europe until Europe is so organised that a strong and united Germany can live within the European fellowship without wishing to provoke war.

There can be no lasting peace with Hitler, because he thinks he is God.

Only one thing can lead to this result—the overthrow of Nazism from inside Germany. The hope of our being able to bring this about by war rests mainly on the fact that the greatest strength of Hitler's appeal so far has lain in his success in winning victories by the mere threat of force, without actual war. As much as the German people reveres Hitler's victories it hates—all but a quite small fraction—the thought of war against Great Britain and France. It remembers the privations of the last war and of the blockade; it is very conscious that it has been living, even in peace, at a standard that allows no margin for further tightening of the belt. It has been led, by continual propaganda, to believe the Western "democracies" to be too effete actually to take up arms against Hitler; and this propaganda can be made to recoil upon those who inspired it, now that it has been proved mistaken. There can be little doubt that up to the last moment Hitler himself, encouraged thereto by the Munich surrender, believed that the politicians of Great Britain and France were too feeble-minded, and too much divided in policy, really to fight; and what he believed his propagandists daily and hourly told the people as certain truth. This *déception* of the German people constitutes to-day our greatest opportunity. . . .

Here, in Great Britain, we see the situation differently. We are very conscious of our own unaggressive intentions, of our intense reluctance to go to war; and we instinctively think of our own privileged position in the world as a right sanctioned by prescription, much as the ordinary rich man

thinks of his property. We see Hitler plainly as a wanton dis-
turber of the peace; a ruthless marauder, a man without re-
straint or conscience. We do not realise easily that, even if
our view of him is correct, Germans, especially under the influence of concentrated propaganda and complete suppression of news and opinion unwelcome to the Nazi regime,
may see the same situation in a very different light. . . .

Three Possible Kinds of Revolutions

It is, however, essential for us to face the fact that there are
now three different possibilities of revolution in Germany.
One—and this, I think, is the revolution which the British
Conservatives would like—is the displacement of Hitler by
his own generals, leading to the reconstruction of a Germany not unlike that which existed before 1914. Such an essentially Conservative revolution, those who favour it hope,
would enable the diplomats to return happily to the tradi-
tions of the nineteenth century, and to make a settlement
which would leave the social system and the social inequal-
ities of Western capitalism miraculously intact. But I rather
think the possibility of this sort of revolution has vanished
now that Josef Stalin has intervened effectively in the affairs
of Central Europe.

The second possible revolution is Communist, or
pseudo-Communist at least. It could come through a transformation of the Nazi State into a State not unlike the Soviet Union. "Brown Bolshevism", someone has called this
type of revolutionary movement; and there are of course elements in German Nazism to which it would be welcome.
It would, on the other hand, be thoroughly unwelcome to
the army leaders, the Prussian aristocrats, and the magnates
of German heavy industry; and it could hardly come about
without a severe internal struggle. I do not dismiss it as impossible; but I greatly doubt its probability, though I expect
Hitler to attempt to represent himself increasingly as the
foe of capitalism and the potential liberator of the down-
trodden masses in the capitalist countries. . . .

What is left? A people's revolution, led by much the
same elements in Germany as controlled the Weimar Republic. A revolution led by Socialists and Liberals and non-
party moderates, with the support of a public opinion weary
of war, regimentation, and totalitarian proceedings generally. Such a revolution would obviously have the backing of

most of the refugees, Jewish or Aryan. It would fit in exactly with the aspirations of the Czechs and probably the Austrians; and it would create in Germany the kind of Government that would be most likely to contribute to the making of a decent peace, and to enter whole-heartedly, given such a peace, into the building up of a federal system in Western and Central Europe. It would be the best of all possible revolutions, if it could be got.

Chronology

April 20, 1889
Hitler is born in the Austrian village of Braunau.

May 1913
Hitler moves to Munich, Germany.

1914–1918
Hitler fights for Germany in World War I.

September 1919
Hitler becomes a member of the right-wing and anti-Semitic German Worker's Party (DAP), which has only a few members. Due to his oratorical skills he soon becomes the speaker at meetings and is in charge of propaganda.

February 1920
DAP becomes the National Socialist German Worker's Party (NSDAP), the Nazi Party.

July 29, 1921
Hitler becomes leader of the Nazi Party.

September 6, 1923
The price of a loaf of bread in Berlin rises to 1 million marks.

November 1923
The price of a bread loaf is at 200 billion marks. People go shopping with wheelbarrows full of paper money.

November 8–9, 1923
The Beer Hall Putsch occurs, an event at which Hitler and his comrades unsuccessfully try to establish a new regime in Munich.

November 15, 1923
A new preliminary currency, the Rentenmark, is introduced.

April–December 1924
After the putsch, Hitler spends time in prison where he writes *Mein Kampf*.

September 14, 1930
The Nazi Party wins 18.3 percent of the vote.

July 31, 1932
New elections are held in which the Nazis win 37.4 percent of the vote.

November 6, 1932
Elections are held once again. The Nazi Party earns only 33.1 percent of the vote.

January 30, 1933
President Paul von Hindenburg appoints Hitler chancellor.

February 27, 1933
The parliament building burns down. Communists are accused of having set the fire.

February 28, 1933
The Reichstag Fire Decree allows Hitler to rule by his own emergency regulations.

March 5, 1933
The Nazis win 43.9 percent of the vote. However, the aim had been to earn the majority.

March 20, 1933
The concentration camp in Dachau opens.

March 23, 1933
Hitler succeeds in suspending the constitution: His Enabling Act wins a majority in the *Reichstag*.

April 1, 1933
A boycott begins against Jewish shops and businesses.

April 7, 1933
The so-called Laws for Reestablishment of the Civil Service bar Jews from positions in state service and at universities.

April 26, 1933
The secret police force Gestapo is established.

May 10, 1933
The Nazis burn thousands of books by Jews and other banned authors.

June 30, 1934
"Night of the Long Knives." Hitler secures his own support in the army by outplaying the leader of his private police force, the Nazi Storm Troopers (SA). Ernst Röhm and other leaders of the SA are assassinated by members of a special police force, the Nazi Security Squadron (SS). Army officials had been concerned that Röhm was planning to incorporate the army into the SA and had given an ultimatum to Hitler. The press claims Röhm had planned to overthrow the Hitler regime.

July 14, 1934
A new law introduces forced sterilization for Germans with congenital disabilities.

August 2, 1934
President Paul von Hindenburg dies. Hitler, already chancellor of Germany, assumes the presidency and appoints himself leader of the Reich. The army must now swear allegiance to him.

September 15, 1935
The Nuremberg Laws declare that Jews can no longer be citizens. Marriage and sexual relations between Jews and non-Jews are illegal.

March 13, 1938
Hitler's army annexes Austria.

September 1, 1939
Hitler's army invades Poland.

September 3, 1939
World War II begins as Britain, France, India, Australia, and New Zealand declare war on Germany.

January 20, 1942
At the Wannsee Conference, Nazi leaders are being informed about the technical details of the Final Solution, the mass extinction of European Jews.

April 30, 1945
With Germany destroyed, Hitler commits suicide in a bunker in Berlin.

For Further Research

Biography

Joachim C. Fest, *Hitler.* Trans. Richard and Clara Winston. New York: Harcourt Brace Jovanovich, 1974.

Brigitte Hamann, *Hitler's Vienna: A Dictator's Apprenticeship.* Trans. Thomas Thornton. New York: Oxford University Press, 1999.

Sydney Jones, *Hitler in Vienna: 1907–1913.* New York: Stein and Day, 1983.

Ian Kershaw, *Hitler.* Harlow, England and New York: Longman, 2001.

Robert Payne, *Life and Death of Adolf Hitler.* New York: Praeger, 1973.

John Toland, *Adolf Hitler.* New York: Doubleday, 1976.

History

Martin Broszat, *The Hitler State: The Foundation and Development of the Internal Structure of the Third Reich.* New York: Longman, 1981.

Alan Bullock, *Hitler: A Study in Tyranny.* New York: Harper & Row, 1962.

Joachim C. Fest, *The Face of the Third Reich: Portraits of the Nazi Leadership.* Trans. Michael Bullock. New York: Da Capo Press, 1999.

Helmut Heiber, *The Weimar Republic.* Trans. W.E. Yuill. Cambridge, MA: Blackwell, 1993.

Konrad Heiden, *The Führer: Hitler's Rise to Power.* Trans. Ralph Manheim. Boston: Houghton Mifflin, 1944.

Adolf Hitler, *Hitler's Table Talk, 1941–1944: His Private Conversations.* Trans. Norman Cameron and R.H. Stevens. Introduced and with a new preface by H.R. Trevor-Roper. New York: Enigma Books, 2000.

————, *Speeches and Proclamations, 1932–1945: The Chronicle of a Dictatorship.* 3 Vols. Ed. Max Domarus. Trans. Mary Fran Gilbert. Wauconda, IL: Bolchazy-Carducci, 1990.

Eberhard Jäckel, *Hitler's World View: A Blueprint for Power.* Trans. Herbert Arnold. Foreword by Franklin L. Ford. Cambridge, MA: Harvard University Press, 1981.

Ian Kershaw, *The "Hitler Myth": Image and Reality in the Third Reich.* New York: Oxford University Press, 1987.

Eberhard Kolb, *The Weimar Republic.* London and Boston: Unwin Hyman, 1988.

Anthony James Nicholls, *Weimar and the Rise of Hitler.* New York: St. Martin's, 1979.

Suzanne Pool and James Pool, *Who Financed Hitler: The Secret Funding of Hitler's Rise to Power, 1919–1933.* New York: Dial Press, 1978.

William L. Shirer, *The Rise and Fall of Adolf Hitler.* New York: Simon & Schuster, 1990.

Louis L. Snyder, *Hitler's Elite: Biographical Sketches of Nazis Who Shaped the Third Reich.* New York: Hippocrene Books, 1989.

Psychology

Fritz Redlich, *Hitler: Diagnosis of a Destructive Prophet.* New York: Oxford University Press, 1999.

Ron Rosenbaum, *Explaining Hitler: The Search for the Origins of His Evil.* New York: Random House, 1998.

George Victor, *Hitler: The Pathology of Evil.* Washington DC: Brassey's, 1998.

Robert Waite, *The Psychopathic God: Adolf Hitler.* New York: BasicBooks, 1977.

Encyclopedias

Wolfgang Benz and Walter H. Pehle, eds., *Encyclopedia of German Resistance to the Nazi Movement.* Trans. Lance W. Garner. New York: Continuum, 1997.

Christian Zentner and Friedemann Bedurftig, eds., *Encyclopedia of the Third Reich.* 2 Vols. Trans. Amy Hackett. New York: Macmillan, 1991.

Index